# *Long-Distance Real Estate Investing*

Find Properties with Real Potential and Achieve Wealth and Cashflow

**ROBERT SMITH**

**PUBLISHED BY: Green Book Publishing LTD**

**58 Warwick Road**

**London W5 5PX**

**First Print 2021**



*Green Book Publishing* ®



**Legal & Disclaimer**

The information contained in this book and its contents is not designed to replace or take the place of any form of medical or professional advice; and is not meant to replace the need for independent medical, financial, legal or other professional advice or services, as may be required. The content and information in this book has been provided for educational and entertainment purposes only.

The content and information contained in this book has been compiled from sources deemed reliable, and it is accurate to the best of the Author's knowledge, information and belief. However, the Author cannot guarantee its accuracy and validity and cannot be held liable for any errors and/or omissions. Further, changes are periodically made to this book as and when needed. Where appropriate and/or necessary, you must consult a professional (including but not limited to your doctor, attorney, financial advisor or such other professional advisor) before using any of the suggested remedies, techniques, or information in this book.

Upon using the contents and information contained in this book, you agree to hold harmless the Author from and against any damages, costs, and expenses, including any legal fees potentially resulting from the application of any of the information provided by this book. This disclaimer applies to any loss, damages or injury caused by the use and application, whether directly or indirectly, of any advice or information presented, whether for breach of contract, tort, negligence, personal injury, criminal intent, or under any other cause of action.

You agree to accept all risks of using the information presented inside this book.

You agree that by continuing to read this book, where appropriate and/or necessary, you shall consult a professional (including but not limited to your doctor, attorney, or financial advisor or such other advisor as needed) before using any of the suggested remedies, techniques, or information in this book.

# Table of Contents

# INTRODUCTION

Is there a difference between an investor who achieves good investments and one who makes bad ones? If one bases themselves on what the financial services industry appears to believe in, then the answer is no. There is no intrinsic difference. All that anyone has to do is to listen to the correct advisers and take in the wisdom provided by the financial companies, and in this way they will be able to generate good investments. However, this ideology is different from what many of us believe.

An individual who interacts with many different kinds of investors finds it easy to trust that there is something hidden about the traits that make some people better investors. Those who constantly run after questionable investments tend to do so because of certain traits of their personality.

However, there is a fixed mindset vs. a growth mindset. Scientists have found that a fixed mindset is common among individuals who have a certain type of intelligence. These people attempt something and succeed without a lot of effort.

On the flip side, those who do not have an intrinsic ability to progress, attempt something, but only succeed with hard work and commitment. They learn an important life lesson: that hard work and effort lead to success. If they work at something, applying a consistent effort, then they will succeed. They learn that if something is hard, that does not mean it cannot be done. It only means it will require more effort and persistence.

By now, it should be clear that this produces specific consequences on the way we invest. There is no point for any of us to get stuck in a cycle of poor investment choices and gains. Most of us go for non-optimal, low – generating investments and find comfort in predictability. One has to work with a bit of effort, choose carefully, and even then success does not occur automatically.

Do you ever look at successful real estate investors and wonder what goes on in their minds? Do you wonder how they think and what makes them tick? Everybody wants success. Chasing it is always long and full of challenges, and we can always turn to those who have already made it for guidance.

First, successful investors do not dwell on mistakes and regrets. If you start to think about your mistakes and regrets, you are sabotaging yourself. Investors will make mistakes, and they may be important mistakes. However, wasting time on regret will not get you anywhere. It only hurts your future prospects because of the fear of your efforts being in vain again.

Secondly, avoid making comparisons: it can be so easy for us, not only investors but people, to begin looking at what everyone else is doing right and to start feeling low. Maybe another investor could be doing better than you. Maybe they cut a better deal than you. Comparison will snatch your joy. There is some gain in learning other people's journeys, but there is no benefit in comparing them. Your luck is yours, and no one's situations are the same. It is impossible to compare them. You will only end up feeling discouraged.

Last but not least, learn to accept that you cannot control everything. None of us has the power to do so. Real estate provides us with more freedom than many other investments. In many different ways, we are the drivers of our luck.

Accepting that there are some things that you have no power over and you will just not be able to command them, is going to take you towards greater success considering that you will not waste energy. Instead of trying to shake the immovable, try dealing with what you can actually control, and handle what you can not as well as you can.

Most investors turn to real estate investment looking for a secondary source of income. There are many ways to earn passively through real estate. Real estate has been proven to be the best channel to earn passively. Earning money from real estate investment is a powerful mean to generate enough capital to live the life one has always dreamt of along with saving enough for your retirement.

This book will help you to learn how to get started as a real estate investor. You will learn why you need to invest in real estate, the different types of real estate devoting, the methods that you can use to invest in real estate, among many other concepts. Even if there are many books written out there about real estate investing, this book is different from the rest because it takes a different approach. First, we address topics in real estate that many books do not discuss. Secondly, we direct ourselves to an investor who is a beginner and who has no experience in real estate investing. In this way, we try to keep everything as simple as possible. Our focus is to help you excel in every field of real estate. Therefore, we present you with factual information that will guide you in every decision that you will take throughout your journey in real estate investing. We hope that you will enjoy reading this book and find it helpful.

# CHAPTER 1 : INVESTING OUT OF STATE

If you are starting in the real estate business, most successful property investors will tell you to invest where you live. This is nice advice because it's difficult to gain deep knowledge of a real estate market if you're not living there. For an experienced real estate investor considering expanding his or her portfolio, long-distance real estate investing is a good option.

**Apply real estate investment tools.** An example of such a tool is the investment property calculator. The tool provides projections of what cash on cash return, rental income, and many more you can expect. Therefore, a real estate investor can review and compare different locations in the comfort of his/her home.

Also, other real estate investment tools help you search for and find properties online.

**Think about getting a real estate partner.** Even with the help of online tools, long-distance real estate investing is still difficult. Maybe you want to buy an investment property in a country or city that you cannot access for one reason or another. In the following case, getting a partner is the most convenient solution. Also, real estate partnerships are great because they generate resources, including experience, networking, knowledge, and capital. Not forgetting to say, they can decrease the general risk of investing in real estate. Therefore, having a partner can simplify your life as a real estate investor.

**Get a professional property management company.** If you are not interested in getting a partner in the city you want to invest in, then your other channel is to allow a property management company to handle the business. These companies will everything, including checking on the investment property, tenant screening, conducting relevant repairs, etc.

## KEY PROBLEMS OF LONG-DISTANCE REAL ESTATE INVESTING

1. Owning an investment property out of state is tiresome if a real estate investor doesn't have enough experience in and knowledge related to real estate investing.
2. There will be a time lag in realizing changes in the real estate market and noticing the nuances of change that may signal the need to sell your investment property before problems arrive.
3. Investing in out of state real estate market is more difficult to handle than in a local market, and it's also very expensive.
4. Hiring the wrong person to manage your property could be a big problem. Real estate

investors have to trust others to look after their rental properties.

**Failing to invest time and enough research analyzing the housing market, the location, and the neighborhood before purchasing the rental property may result in huge losses.**

# CHAPTER 2: INTERNET IS A BOON

No individual can ever succeed entirely without the help of others. People need people, and that is just how nature and the universe designed and willed it to be. Therefore, looking for the best people to collaborate with is much more important than looking for your deals.

"People facilitate properties to generate the moolah, never the other way around! Always remember, deals do not own people; people own deals! Properties are properties of people!"

To fulfill your urgent need for people, you simply ought to connect and interconnect, interact and establish these relationships with other people. In short, you need to network, meet, mingle, and know others for the simple purpose of creating mutual support or assistance towards moving one another forward.

Networking does not need to be a formal or methodical activity. Instead, your daily interactions with people should be integral to your networking strategy. Let networking be your lifestyle, your way of life!

The real estate industry, as always, has its own share of the good times and the bad times—the equally interesting rise and fall of fortunes. Back in 2006, just before the housing financial crisis, the membership of the National Association of Realtors (NAR) hit an all-time record high of a little below 1.5 million.

During and after the bursting of the housing bubble, however, it nosedived dramatically to its rock bottom of less than a million members in 2012. A rejuvenated membership had only picked up the slack a couple of years later; and since then, it has kept on increasing steadily, reaching 1.3 million members as of 2017.

Indeed, the current competition is becoming fiercer than ever. Nowadays, you ought to step up your efforts to survive and thrive, especially amidst the changing times and the fast-paced advancements in technological innovations.

Although real estate brokers/marketers remain the key players in the ***property buying process***, property investors increasingly prefer performing more of the legwork on the Internet before associating with the gurus. According to a 2017 NAR study, more than 90% of investors use the Web to launch their property-hunting quest, creating the urgency for real estate brokers and marketers to engage in a more dynamic presence online.

If you are not engaging in an active networking online, then you are definitely missing out on half the life of the industry. To set yourself distinctively apart from the pack, you will just truly require both proficient online and offline real estate marketing skills and strategies. The following is a compilation of the most sensible real estate marketing ideas and strategies of the times to help you conquer the real estate marketing competition:

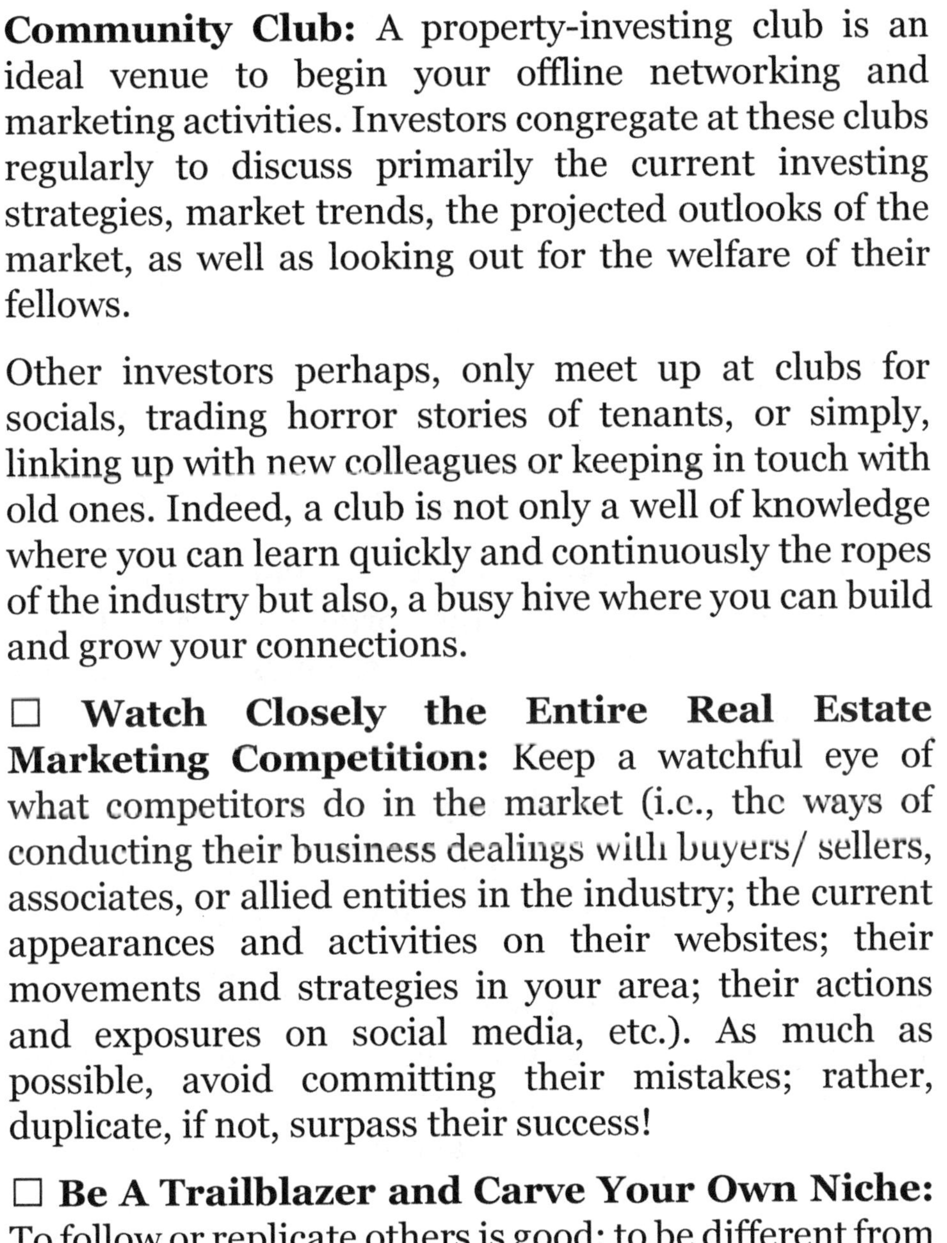

☐ **Join a Real Estate Professional Investors' Community Club:** A property-investing club is an ideal venue to begin your offline networking and marketing activities. Investors congregate at these clubs regularly to discuss primarily the current investing strategies, market trends, the projected outlooks of the market, as well as looking out for the welfare of their fellows.

Other investors perhaps, only meet up at clubs for socials, trading horror stories of tenants, or simply, linking up with new colleagues or keeping in touch with old ones. Indeed, a club is not only a well of knowledge where you can learn quickly and continuously the ropes of the industry but also, a busy hive where you can build and grow your connections.

☐ **Watch Closely the Entire Real Estate Marketing Competition:** Keep a watchful eye of what competitors do in the market (i.e., the ways of conducting their business dealings with buyers/ sellers, associates, or allied entities in the industry; the current appearances and activities on their websites; their movements and strategies in your area; their actions and exposures on social media, etc.). As much as possible, avoid committing their mistakes; rather, duplicate, if not, surpass their success!

☐ **Be A Trailblazer and Carve Your Own Niche:** To follow or replicate others is good; to be different from the rest is better. If brewing marketing competition truly exists in your area, consider becoming a trailblazer and excelling at treading your path.

Make a name for yourself by establishing your expertise in a specific niche. Perhaps, you might want to stand out as the most trusted and reliable realtor for small families with toddlers, young urban professionals, divorcees, retirees, or whatever.

☐ **Design a Professionally Impressive Business Card:** While most old-fashioned realty marketing aspects are fading away quickly, the business card remains an essential staple in the real estate industry. Create an awesome, professional-looking business card and dispense it around all your circles of influence.

☐ **Set Up and Establish Your Personal Brand Presence Online:** Open the portal of the World Wide Web. Your entry leads you to vast fields of networking and marketing opportunities—social media, online community forums, communication apps, the blogosphere, and what have you.

Explore and exploit these free networking and marketing services to the greatest possible advantage with respect to your property-investing career. Foremost, ensure creating your social media accounts on all the giant networking sites (i.e., Facebook, Google+, Pinterest, Twitter, Tumbler, and even Instagram or Vero if you take countless snapshots of houses/properties).

You need not be present at most times on every network; focusing on a single or a couple is much better than becoming non-existent on all sites. Be constantly active in your sites by interacting regularly with users, posting your activities, promoting your properties, and sharing good press, contents, or emotional stories with compelling copies and powerful audio/visual elements.

Remember, social media is all about creating and building relationships. Therefore, beware of using it as your advertising platform. Your networking trick should rather be spending a portion of your time growing solid relationships while making an impression of yourself as someone with knowledge in your craft.

If you want to advertise, include social media paid ads in the saddle. Dish out a budget for social media paid ads like Facebook ads, which are generally the most effective channel to get in front of your target audience.

☐ **Participate In Real Estate Investing Community Forums:** Similar to community clubs, these forums are online communities participated by professional realtors and realty investors. They network with one another at all times of the day. Usually, their networking activities are about sharing relevant and significant information about the market/industry, as well as helping one another to learn, grow, and prosper.

It is noteworthy that networking in these forums must never be about what you can get something out of them, but rather, how you can contribute to the conversations.

Thus, you can help yourself learn by just reading between the lines of the dialogues.

☐ **Create and Develop an Outstanding Website:** Most consumers nowadays prefer doing the bulk of the legwork themselves online whenever they make major decisions on purchasing various products or availing specific services (which both include buying real estate and using realty services). Take their cue; build one!

Owning a website reflects professionalism and seriousness of doing business in the industry. Not only will your business website address the needs of people but also, it serves your interests in networking and marketing your business.

Building a great website is neither difficult nor expensive. Being terrible at technology is not a valid excuse in today's technology-friendly world. You should only brush up more on user experience (UX) design skills rather than site architecture technology.

Essentially, your site is your storefront to your business. Thus, it must require looking spic and span, professional, organized, easy to navigate, mobile-friendly, and alluring to attract more people flocking to your site. Make everything simple but sleek.

In your site, you should create irresistible contents that offer to capture your prospects or leads. Ensure your copy to include locally oriented keywords so that homebuyers searching online in your area can run across your content.

You should also add the pertinent social sharing buttons on your site. Home shoppers are always more than eager to share top picks of housing pics with their family and friends.

Lastly, you should make yourself easily available and contacted. Ideally, create an attention-grabbing 'contact us' page on your site; also, place your contact details on every page in your site.

☐ **Build Your 'Google My Business' Website:** Attract new sets of clientele and opportunities with a free business listing by setting up your Google My Business website. Your listing is a location-based page that appears right down people's alley when they search for businesses or services like yours on both Google Search and Google Maps.

Usually, homebuyers will use Google Map to search the address of a property and view the property's photos. They will also use the map's Street View feature to get a feel of the locality, see the proximities of landmarks, businesses, or places of interests, and more ideally, take on a virtual tour of the entire property. Hence, always have the user experience in mind by ensuring their easy access to all the aforementioned information to your page. Ensure also to have great eye-catching photos and smooth virtual tours.

☐ **Get Aboard on Pinterest Boards:** Optimize your activity at Pinterest by creating Pinterest boards. They are most useful for providing high-resolution images and comprehensive visual information about your specific property listings.

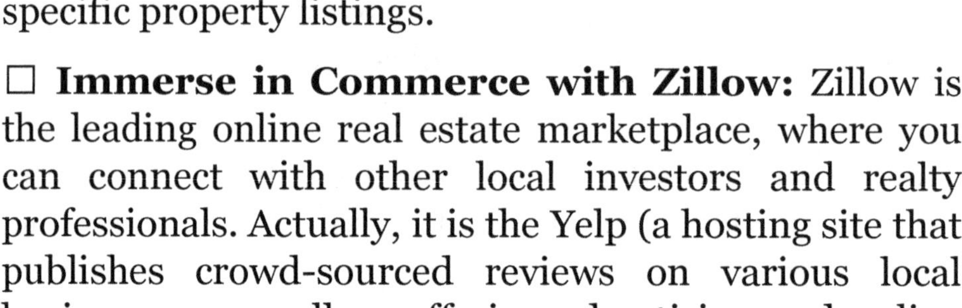

☐ **Immerse in Commerce with Zillow:** Zillow is the leading online real estate marketplace, where you can connect with other local investors and realty professionals. Actually, it is the Yelp (a hosting site that publishes crowd-sourced reviews on various local businesses, as well as offering advertising and online reservation services) of real estate marketing.

At Zillow, you can search for your most desired deals from its humongous database, which contains infinite numbers of rental and for-sale listings. You can also compare property values by using the site's property valuation tool, Zestimate.

Zillow also offers abilities to advertise your properties and being an agent on their site. This could somehow be a bit pricey, but taking into account the enormous role Zillow plays in the industry, it is certainly your best bet. For, after all, the site accounts for more than 50% online traffic for all searches about real estate.

Like Yelp, Zillow allows its users to review and rate real estate agents. Hence, wear your best smile and keep on racking up your rating. Solid star-ratings will greatly help to increase your leads, as well as capturing them to close a deal.

☐ **Apply A Leveraged Call-Tracking System:** Most property buyers reach over the telephone when availing the services of a realtor or placing an appointment to inspect a property. Usually, these calls arise from your paid search campaigns (i.e., social media paid ads or pay-per-click ads).

From these calls and their transpired conversations, you will be able to track or know which of your ads or the keywords you use are driving all these calls. Apply this call-tracking system to devise and develop your real estate marketing funnel.

☐ **Execute Marketing via Direct Mail/Email:** Regardless if you are buy-and-hold, flipper, or wholesaler, your investing business relies not only on looking for great deals but also on having a steady supply of prospects for those deals. For a huge number of investors, direct mailing is their primary source of leads.

Mailing, either direct or electronic, is simply sending letters, newsletters, postcards, etc. to these targeted prospects, with the hope that a certain percentage of the recipients respond. The concept of mail campaigns is to let your audience build an awareness of your brand, business, product, or service over the course of time. A response could lead you to be the ultimate solution to their pressing needs.

Build your mailing list either by procuring public records from your local assessor or hiring an online outfit (i.e., ListSource). Obtaining public records is free while using an online service can save you time; hence, keep your objectives in mind when creating your mailing list.

In addition, never fail to include in your list those absentee property owners, as well as owners of abandoned properties, apartment buildings, pre-foreclosed or foreclosed properties, expired listings, and **'probates'** (properties undergoing distribution or transfer to heirs of the deceased owner). More often than not, these types of property owners will be leading you to fantastic opportunities and land great deals.

They neither want to hold on any longer with their assets or care about spending and maintaining their properties. As a result, they just wish to sell their properties at a discount.

With a changing market, update your list every six months to rid out those unresponsive ones while giving room for new leads. The frequency by which you send your mail and the duration of your campaign varies depending on the marketing funnel you set up and the investing method you are engaging.

☐ **Exercise Post-Closing Marketing Techniques:** Your relationships with your clients must be never-ending, even after a close. Let them remember you, your service, and the entire fruitful experience shared.

You may send them a local care package or restaurant gift cards or theater or movie tickets, etc. Always stay in touch with your past buyers to maintain goodwill. You may send greeting cards, holiday or anniversary cards, etc. to help them recall you.

Never mind the cost; do not even perceive it as public relations tactics. Instead, mind to share your blessings.

Besides, your main intent is making them remember your person and personal brand. These items are just a minuscule of the overflowing returns ahead like continuing business deals or precious referrals.

Testimonials from previous clients are tremendous trust signals. Find ways to let them endorse you without soliciting directly. Real people supporting and showing your services to the world is an indirect marketing to gain more potential clients. Make the most out of these testimonials and endorsements by posting them strategically on your site while sharing them every now and then on social media networks.

As you may see, the ideas aforementioned are not expansive and do not even include other options possible. Fact is that an entire book can cover each marketing concept and technique. Nonetheless, the book presents you with the most commonly used real estate marketing strategies today.

The real estate marketing process is not really a simple and smooth-sailing activity. One important aspect to keep in mind, especially when you are still getting started, is to put your focus on just a single or a couple of marketing strategies. Work hard to implement them carefully. At the same time, monitor the results.

As soon as you found what worked out, stick with it. If you plan to generate more leads, try to expand your newfound successful strategy. Alternatively, move on to practice another marketing technique.

Just the same, not all real estate marketing strategies produce effective results. For this reason, your vital key is to maintain accurate records and test continuously your marketing campaigns.

# CHAPTER 3: UNDERSTANDING THE REAL ESTATE MARKET

This chapter is intended for those folks who already have purchased their first home and are looking to buy an additional property or have some cash they would like to put to work.

As I mentioned in the introduction, real estate can generally outperform other asset classes in the long run. While everyone dreams of getting into an IPO that skyrockets and makes millions overnight, the chances that investing in stocks will make you rich is slim, at best. The volatility in stocks may be too much for some to stomach.

Now, this doesn't mean that you shouldn't invest in stocks. It's important to note that there are no safe investments out there, but there are some that pose less risk when compared to others.

Considering that the stock market is too volatile and investment accounts in your neighborhood bank can't keep up with inflation, your best bet is real estate. It's true that there are other asset classes out there such as precious metals, fine art, or even commodities like copper, corn, or oil, but those are not the type of assets which can make your nest egg grow and provide you with a source of passive income.

If you're just considering how you can make a couple of extra bucks, and protect your wealth at the same time, then a second property is definitely a good choice.

This section will take a hard and honest look at investing in real estate.

## HOW TO MAKE MONEY WITH RENTAL PROPERTIES

This is the promised land with real estate investors.

Unless you are a multi-million-dollar developer building malls and skyscrapers, you are most likely looking at jumping into a second property, and perhaps a third, and so on. Most folks are content with having a second, cash-producing property, but for those who are more ambitious, it's possible to keep adding more properties.

But before moving on, there is a key factor that you need to keep in mind before going about investments: discipline.

Discipline is a crucial factor in making money with rental properties as you must not think of a second property as an ATM. In fact, whatever profits you make, part of them will have to be reinvested into the property at some point. In short, you need to network, meet, mingle, and know others for the simple purpose of creating mutual support or assistance towards moving one another forward.

Networking does not need to be a formal or methodical activity. Instead, your daily interactions with people should be integral to your networking strategy. Let networking be your lifestyle, your way of life!

The real estate industry, as always, has its own share of the good times and the bad times—the equally interesting rise and fall of fortunes. Back in 2006, just before the housing financial crisis, the membership of the National Association of Realtors (NAR) hit an all-time record high of a little below 1.5 million.

During and after the bursting of the housing bubble, however, it nosedived dramatically to its rock bottom of less than a million members in 2012. A rejuvenated membership had only picked up the slack a couple of years later; and since then, it has kept on increasing steadily, reaching 1.3 million members as of 2017.

Indeed, the current competition is becoming fiercer than ever. Nowadays, you ought to step up your efforts to survive and thrive, especially amidst the changing times and the fast-paced advancements in technological innovations.

For example, when one tenant moves out, you may need to put on a fresh coat of paint and new carpets in. You might also run into larger expenses such as roofing and HVAC systems. So, it's always best to set some of that money aside every month.

In order to ensure this discipline, I recommend having a separate bank account specifically for the property. For example, your tenant may choose to deposit their rent into that account. So, you would only need to withdraw the money needed to cover the mortgage payments and taxes. The rest stays in that account. Over time, it will add up.

One other very important expense to consider is that when tenants move out, you may not rent the property out immediately. In fact, it may sit there for a month or two. In the meantime, you need to cover the mortgage and utility payments. This is money that you will get back when you rent the property out again, but it is a common pitfall with rental properties.

In addition, you might have tenants who fall behind on their rent. But, you are on the hook for making the mortgage payments. So, this is where having that extra cushion can keep you from paying these expenses out of your own pocket.

Now, I know what you are thinking: if real estate is supposed to be a "safer" investment, then why am I exposed to so much risk?

Naturally, no investment is devoid of risk. There is always a risk attached to all investments. There are no exceptions. These reflections are intended to help you manage risk and be aware of what you are getting yourself into. Consequently, your ability to foresee these risks will enable you to keep your head above water and generate profits from your rental property.

So then, what is the point of investing in rental properties if I may not be able to actually make money off of it?

An erroneous view on investments is that successful investments produce cash. Some folks get it completely wrong by thinking that rental properties will allow them to quit their jobs and enable them to live off that income. And yes, that is possible if you have enough properties producing enough cash per month in order to sustain your lifestyle.

The reality though is that investments serve two purposes: one is to make your initial investment grow over time and eventually leave you with more money than you put it. The other purpose is to protect your money's purchasing power over time.

This second point is very important, and it is the reason why you can't just leave your money under the mattress. In the modern economy, inflation will slowly eat away at your money.

How does that work?

Let's assume a 2% annual inflation rate. Inflation is essentially the increase of prices on the goods and services you consume. This is why you pay more now than your parents did at your age. So, if you let $100 sit under your mattress, after one year, your $100 can buy $98 worth of goods and services. Now, imagine the effect that this can have over 5 or 10 years.

When you put your money into real estate, you can hedge your investment by raising rents every time you get a new tenant. Of course, you can't hike up the rent too high because you need to take the market into consideration. If rents become stagnant, then you can't hike up the rent too much because renters simply won't pay it. But if the market is hot, then you can hike up your rent in tandem with the market.

Also, you will commonly see and hear how investing in real estate is a great way for you to save up for retirement. Again, you would ideally have paid off any and all mortgages by the time you retire. That means that the cash you get from your rents will go straight into your pocket. This, combined with other savings and investments, will allow you to retire within your means. But younger folks should be keen on keeping their jobs and sustaining that income.

At the end of the day financial freedom is not quitting your job and spending your time traveling around the world; financial freedom is having the option to quit your job whenever you want. It's not that you're actually going to do it, but if you wanted to take time off, you have that choice. And, real estate is a means to achieve that goal.

In the following section, we're going to take a deeper look at securing financing for a second property.

## BUILDING A RENTAL PROPERTY

In this section, we'll consider the case of purchasing land and then building on it, or, tearing down a property and building a new one.

In short, I can tell you that's a bad idea. Unless you buy a property in a city that's offering you some kind of incentive for building a new property or knocking down old ones and rebuilding, I would advise against this.

Why?

Well, construction costs can spike and zap your potential profits. Just the cost associated with having plans drawn up, construction licenses, zoning rights, and the cost of materials and labor could outweigh future gains.

I would be comfortable doing this in one of two cases:

**1. You have bought the land in cash and have taken out a loan for construction; or**

**2. You have a mortgage on the land a have the cash to build.**

If you are financing both the land and construction, you are setting yourself up for trouble.

One way you could try to go about this is to find a town such as Lincoln, Kansas. This town has a total population of 3,500 residents and is looking to boost their population. They are offering free land and a 10-year tax break, but the catch is that you need to build on the property within 18 months of receiving the land. If you have the stomach for such an endeavor, then programs such as these could provide excellent returns in the long run.

Another word of caution here extends to "flippers." These folks look for distressed properties or "fixer-uppers", take care of the repairs needed and then put them back on the market at a markup. If you've seen these folks on TV, they have one thing in common: they do the work themselves.

Why?

Because they save a ton on a labor and they split the profits. If you've ever seen any of these shows, these folks always pass up on the houses that need a new foundation or roof. They stick to replacing doors and redoing cabinets. Even a new furnace will send these guys running out the door. Such major renovations will almost certainly zap their profits.

The best rental properties are the kind that don't require significant repairs and are essentially move-in ready. While it's normal to paint walls and put in new carpet, replacing a roof is far too much to be done on a rental property. In fact, most investors look to newer developments in order to find their investment. Granted, the price will be higher, but you would save a lot more in the long run. Again, unless you have the time and the stomach for taking on a project, it's best to stay clear of fixer-uppers.

Then, there are contractors. We'll be taking a deeper look at contractors in the next chapter. But for now, it's important to consider that not all contractors are made equal. Some are phenomenal, and some not so much. This is why I stress the importance of doing repairs yourself in case you are considering the possibility of flipping a property.

Anyone who's ever been through a major renovation will tell you that they went over budget due to unforeseen expenses along the way. If you are investing in your primary residence with your family's comfort in mind, then so be it.

With rental properties, your focus should be to stay in compliance with building codes and maintaining a decent property for your renters. That is why flipping properties is simply not worth the hassle, not to mention building one from scratch. The risks and costs far outweigh the benefits.

## ARE YOU READY FOR A SECOND PROPERTY?

Now, there are two main conditions in which I would advise someone to go for a second property:

**1. You have already paid off your first property; or**

**2. You have a significant increase in your income.**

Let's talk about the first condition.

If you have already paid off your first property, or if you inherited the property in which you are currently living, then it would make sense to either rent your current property and move into the new one or rent out the second property. Now, we're not talking about "flipping houses" as it is commonly referred to those who buy and resell properties. Here, we're talking about jumping into a cash-producing property, which in the best of cases will pay off the mortgage on it, and also put some extra cash in your pocket.

The second condition refers to those cases where you change jobs and your income increases significantly, or if you started a business and it has become very successful. In either case, the first thing you need to ask yourself is if this increase in income is sustainable.

Why, you ask?

Let's say that your business has really taken off. You went from making 20–30k a year to perhaps hundreds of thousands. The result of a successful business or perhaps some temporary spike in demand for your product or services? The answer to that will determine if you are safe to invest.

Also, inheritances don't count. Unless you inherit an annuity or other cash-producing assets such as stocks or other rental properties, don't bet your inheritance on a property. It could be that an inheritance could serve you as a down payment. In that case, you would need to be aware that you can afford the new mortgage and costs associated.

If you answer "yes" to either one of the previous questions, and you are certain that your income will cover the expenses associated to the first property and the costs associated to the second, then you have the green light to get the ball rolling.

However, a word of caution first.

A beachfront condo that you will be using once or twice a year does not qualify as an investment. If you are buying a property on the cheap in hopes of it gaining value, then you really need to visit your doctor and make sure you have a clean bill of health because such speculative investments are not for the faint of heart.

An investment counts only when you can make money from it. If you buy anything, whatever it may be, and hold on to it until its value increases, then you are treading into speculation territory. Speculators have been known to be wiped out when the market takes a downturn. This is why a sound investment strategy does not devote large amounts of capital into speculation. Think of it as a poker game. You wouldn't bet your house on a poker game, right?

Consequently, your second property should be intended as a rental property. You must not become attached to it because if the market tanks or if the market takes off, you may have to either get rid of it or sell it and collect the cash.

But if it should happen, then you need to be ready to get rid of it as quickly as you can. And yes, you can sell a home even if it's got a long-term rental contract on it.

If the best should happen and a property takes off, you could sell it and make a killing on it. In this case, it's your decision. But I believe it's best to sell on the highs and not on the lows. Some folks hang on to properties too long and end up missing on valuable opportunities. As such, please don't think that your homework is done when you move into a new property or close on your second one. Your homework should be ongoing since you are out to protect your family's best interest.

Checking on market trends is a lot easier than you think. You can drive around your neighborhood as you usually do and see if there are any "for sale" signs up. You can check your zip code on Zillow to see what's available and what the asking price is.

One such example is some friends who live in Toronto, Canada. The market in Toronto got to be so blazing hot. A friend's dad ended up selling his home because he was constantly badgered by realtors. In the end, he got an offer he couldn't refuse. He sold on the high, bought himself a larger property outside the city and put his profits to work in his own business.

That is a once-in-a-lifetime deal, but it could happen to you if you are able to recognize the trends and see where such trends may lead. In order to achieve this, your study of markets needs to be consistent. That is why I am always looking at Zillow, MLS listings, or even Craigslist. You never know what you might find.

In the following section, we are going to take a better look at how you can make money off rental properties.

## HOW TO SECURE FINANCING FOR A SECOND PROPERTY

In a nutshell, this is the same process as securing the financing for a first home.

That should leave you in great standing with your lender unless you happened to run into credit card trouble or some other type of credit issues. But generally speaking, you should be in good standing. The lender will make you go through the motions again, but it will mostly be paperwork.

In the event that you inherited your first property and have never applied for a mortgage, then you would fall into the same category as a first-time buyer. The difference is that this second property would not necessarily become your primary residence.

Another important difference is that the purchase of this second property would produce income. Remember when I said that bank will look at ALL your sources of income? Well, the bank will consider the rent you could produce from the second property, or if you intend to rent the first one, they will take that into account. Therefore, just the rent from either property might be enough to get you off the ground. If you can muster up a 20% down payment plus closing costs, you will be well on your way to riding off into the sunset.

As long as you are in good standing with your lender, you can apply for a third property so long as you can produce the 20% down plus closing and provide enough proof of income.

If you have a longer-term rental such as a single-family home, then you would be on the hook for declaring this income as a part of your total income. The good part is that you can deduct rental expenses such as insurance, mortgage interest, and even property taxes.

At this point, I hope you are getting the same idea as I am: the best rental properties are those properties you can rent out for a short period of time, typically less than a week because you can declare it as a second home.

Take the example of a beach house or a condo. You can rent this out for a few days, and the IRS won't come breathing down your neck.

This last trick is the reason why property owners who rent out their places on Airbnb don't get nailed with taxes. In fact, I've known some owners who have taken out mortgages on a second place specifically to put it up on Airbnb. It's the same thing that some folks do when they buy a car and then use it to drive for Uber.

Tip: if you are looking to sell your investment property, make it your primary residence, even if you don't actually live there, before you put it on the market. When the sale goes through, you would be selling your primary residence and therefore collect a tax-free profit of up to $500,000. If your profit goes beyond that amount, then you would be on the hook for taxes in excess of $500,000. If the profit that you make is, say, $100,000. Then you are free and clear.

These tips should work in every state. However, I always recommend folks to have a chat with their accountant and realtor before making a play. Remember: it always pays to do your homework.

## RISKS INVOLVED IN OWNING A RENTAL PROPERTY

In the previous section, we took a very deep look at the risk involved in building a property. The conclusion to that section was to stay away from building unless you have the cash flow to offset any unexpected expenses. Even then, there is a clear risk in having your profit wiped out.

However, there are additional risks that come with owning rental properties.

Firstly, there is always the risk that tenants will damage the property. This is quite common and can jack up maintenance costs when tenants move out. This type of damage goes beyond the usual fresh coat of paint or new carpet that needs to be put in. In some cases, larger repairs need to be made. For example, broken fixtures, tiles, and even flooring can become costly. Also, there are cases where children can punch holes in drywall and pets can cause serious damage.

If a property has been seriously damaged, the repairs can be deducted from the renter's security deposit. However, it's not that simple. The damage needs to be properly documented and estimates need to be drawn up by contractors in order to justify the deduction. This could pose a complicated situation especially if the tenant chooses to fight it.

Insurance on rental properties does set limits on how much damage you can claim on it, but it can keep you from having to cover unexpected repairs out of pocket. However, this is an additional expense attached to the property. But have no fear, you can claim it as a deduction.

Another serious risk is having a renter default on their payments. While this would trash the renter's credit, a bankruptcy court can clear the obligation on the part of the renter. That leaves the owner with no means of getting that money back. Once again, insurance can cover lost rent up to a certain maximum. This varies according to the insurer and it certainly pays to shop around.

If you choose to go the way of short-term rentals, collecting fees upfront is the best way to protect yourself from not getting paid. In a sense, it works just like a hotel. Platforms such as Airbnb have protection built in to ensure that even if someone flakes on a booking, the owner is still compensated for that loss.

There is one other very important reason for insurance on rental properties: accidents. There is always the possibility that an accident could occur on the property. For instance, someone trips down the stairs and decides to sue the landlord for negligence. Insurance would keep you from bearing the brunt of the lawsuit. Even if the landlord is held liable, insurance can kick in and protect you from being wiped out. You may think that's a bit extreme, but it happens.

As for the major risks involved in owning rental property, the biggest risk is associated with financials.

For example, being unable to cover the mortgage payments, particularly if the property sits empty. This may seem extreme, but given certain situations, it can.

I recall the aftermath of hurricane Hermine in 2016. This hurricane flooded great parts of Southeast Florida. While this hurricane wasn't as destructive as Sandy in New York or hurricane Katrina in New Orleans, it was strong enough to damage over 200 homes and displaced over a thousand people. It was enough to ruin the lives of many homeowners. Even those that did have insurance needed to wait weeks before anything was done. In the meantime, possessions and were lost not to mention lost earning on rental properties.

What about hurricane Harvey in Houston? This hurricane decimated the market. Many homes that had been up for sale were basically stranded due to the flooding. The homes that weren't flooded dropped in value practically overnight. Many buyers were scared to purchase anything in that area out of fear another similar event. Those that decided to sell had to short their properties just so they could leave the area as fast as they could.

As you can see by the previous examples, natural disasters represent a considerable risk, particularly to investments. The California forest fires in 2018 leveled million-dollar mansions. And even with insurance payouts, many celebrities were struggling to rebuild their palaces. This zone has now been deemed a high-risk area by the State of California. What this means is that many of the homes destroyed by the fires are not going to be rebuilt because the insurance companies simply won't cover them anymore. Now, that's a tough loss.

Once again, I stress the fact need for doing your homework. The time you put into researching a given area and meeting with your realtor will save you loads of headaches down the road.

Lastly, one final thought in this section: try to avoid "hot" markets as much as possible. When a given market gains momentum, homebuyers flock to these areas looking for a great property. This only drives up prices due to the effects of supply and demand. If you happen to recognize this pattern, you need to stay away from it. When property prices are jacked up, then you run the risk of overpaying. That risk can translate into a loss when the market cools and prices settle back down. You'll be stuck with a mortgage that is costing you more than what the property is worth.

An easy way of looking at this is to go in the opposite direction of the crowds. This will allow you to see the forest for threes. Avoid the fear of missing out. If you miss on a market, that's fine. You just have to keep an eye out for the next big boom. If you get in early, you can cash out quite well.

Tip: If you are open to buying property in areas away from your residence. Make sure the new property is located in an area you are comfortable traveling to. I have seen cases of people living in Wisconsin, yet they have properties in Arizona. This can become very inconvenient after a while. You need to be able to supervise what's going on with your property. Otherwise, you may not be able to react appropriately should anything happen. One recommendation I generally make is to buy properties in areas where you have family and friends you can trust to keep an eye on it for you.

# CHAPTER 4: ADDING PEOPLE TO YOUR REAL ESTATE TEAM

## DEAL FINDER

As a matter of fact, several rental companies and rental websites have popped up to help real estate investors in recent times. But, concurrently, as the number of rental websites continues to increase, it has become more problematic for people not only to identify rental properties but even to understand what is the best channel to use in order to detect the rental properties that real estate investors might be interested in.

## AGENTS

One of the biggest challenges in selling a house is to find the right agent to work with. While it makes the whole experience less stressful, you need to make sure that you have the right one; otherwise, the issue will be too tough.

The real estate agent you choose needs to have a few features that will make them the best for your needs:

- Don't choose the agent based on the experience they have; rather you need to choose someone that you have a good rapport with. Although experience is a good indication to have, it isn't everything. You are going to spend a lot of time with the agent, so you need to really bond. Make sure the person is relatable as well as real. You are choosing the agent for you, not the property. The agent needs to be a good talker and a negotiator as well.

- Look at the chemistry. When you decide to work with an agent, try to look at the chemistry that you have with them. Get a few real estate agents and gauge their honesty and trust, so that you know that you will work well with them.
- Seek referrals. Despite having the technology, you still need real referrals from people that have interacted with real estate agents before. The right referrals need to come from people that are close to you or professional contacts. Ask homeowners which agent they worked with, and then create a list that you can use.
- The real estate agent you choose needs to have your interests at heart all the time. The agent needs to be transparent and honest about what they are looking to help you achieve, and they will also make sure you get what you go out to in the first place. The agent will try so much to work within your goals and not within his goals. Make sure you ask a lot of questions before you can commit to this professional relationship.

## FINDING LENDERS

- Adequate support. Before you engage a real estate agent, you need to do your research first before you move onto the next thing. When looking at the agent, you need to consider whether they have a team behind them and if they have a customer care team that will respond to your queries and needs. Remember that the agent you are working with doesn't work with you alone – he works with other people as well. And since the logistics of selling a property are daunting, you need to have support all the time.

- Understands risk. You need to work with a real estate agent that understands the risks of selling a house and will throw out any flattery. You want to work with an agent that is realistic about what to expect and is able to mitigate risk in a proper way. Pay close attention to how the agent uses data to tell you about what is happening in the market at all times. The agent needs to tell you about the risk analysis of the decision to buy as well as what to expect in the crowded market that you seek to penetrate.

- Core values. When it comes to making progress with the sale, you need to find a good person that will make sure you enjoy the best experience ever. This boils down to the core values that the agent has – including truthfulness, honesty, and many more.

- Track record. Real estate agents don't just show up out of nowhere; they come from experience and making sure that they do things the right way. Make sure you look at what the top brokers do, then compare to what your agent is doing before you take them up.

## HIRING A PROPERTY MANAGER

- Follow your gut feeling. When you decide to make a decision, usually you follow your gut feeling to the latter. This means that you need to meet with a few agents and then follow your gut feeling when it comes to making the right decision. First, look to see if the agent has done business before and if they are recommended by many people. Next, check your gut feeling, if it tells you that things are right, and then this is the right person for the task.

- Trust is vital. Make sure the agent you choose is trustworthy. When you begin a conversation with the agent, try and look at what they answer when you talk to them. Many successful agents have gone to where they are because they are trustworthy. Make sure you have mutual respect and trust between the two of you to work best.

Passion. Passion drives commitment. When you have an agent that isn't passionate about selling your property, the chances are that you will struggle to find a buyer. On the other hand, if you find an agent that is ready to work with you the right way, then you will see the results fast enough.

# CHAPTER 5: MANAGING OUT OF STATE REAL ESTATE

A lot of investment related decisions will be based on common sense factors as well, a fact which you will note, is constantly reiterated throughout the contents of this book. Knowing when to take a risk, and understanding the value (or not) of buying low simply because property is being offered at a low price, is based on numerous common sense factors. For example, if you were offered property at a suspiciously low price, and bought it on impulse, only to realize that fixing and redecorating it would cost you double your investment amount, which would constitute a bad investment.

- Get your finances in order first. The most common misconception in real estate is the idea of investing with no cash. This is typically not true, and if you are planning to invest far from the state, you must have the financial capability to buy and manage. Ensure you have enough savings if you want to try long-distance real estate investing and reap huge profits in the long run.

- Watch out for state laws regarding real estate investors and landlords. The main purpose of long-distance real estate investing is to get a nice ROI and earn high profits in return. Before you dive in on investment property, ensure you pay attention to the State Laws and property taxes regarding your real estate business. If the taxes are too high, they may eat into your profits and make long-distance real estate investing bad news for your bottom line.

- Do not discount the price to rent ratio. One of the easiest ways to take advantage of the location for real estate investing is to apply the price to rent ratio across different real estate markets to determine the capitalization rate, the occupancy rate, and the rental income. The price to rent ratio provides real estate investors with a great idea of where to purchase real estate for profit.

- Determine the correct professional property management team. Treat real estate such as business, and place a high value in selecting the best people to run your business.

- Deep research, analysis, and being informed. Don't crunch numbers only on the investment property you are planning. Analyze your profit potential and approximate how your prospective investment numbers suit the local housing market.

- Gain enough experience and knowledge before diving in long-distance real estate investing. Again, if you're buying your first investment property, it is important to invest where you live. As you gain experience and gain the right knowledge, you can branch out and consider long-distance real estate investing in expanding your real estate investment portfolio.

Don't cut corners, and don't leave a bad process to fend for itself. It might cost you time and money in the long run, and it may even topple your business if you aren't careful.

# CHAPTER 6 :FINDING THE RIGHT PROPERTY

Here are some factors you must consider before closing in on the right property:

- **Location** – It is wise to choose a property in a location that is close to where you live because you will visit it multiple times during the rehabilitation period.
- **Good neighborhood** – There is no point in making a home look good if the neighborhood is not well-maintained or is prone to high crime rates and other issues.
- **Proximity to amenities** – Ensure there are good amenities such as parks, shopping areas, school, and restaurants within reasonable distances from the property.
- **Market conditions** – Look up the market conditions of the locality and check out how long any property listings of the area were sitting on the market before being sold.
- **Structural issues** – If the property you choose has structural problems such as poor foundation strength, sinking floors, etc., then not only will your rehab costs go up considerably, you might also need new licenses and permits to complete the renovation. It would be wise, therefore, to

avoid properties which have significant structural issues.

- **Ensure your repairs add value to the property** – Your fix-and-flip properties should ideally get repairs that add value to them. It could be in the form of large closets for increased storage, updated kitchens and bathrooms, and a few cosmetic changes that can give a face-lift to the home. Such value-additions attract buyers.
- **Focus on the size of the property** – The larger the property, the better for fix-and-flip investment strategy. Alterations to the floor plans, removing load-bearing walls for more room, and other such things can be easily accomplished during the rehabilitation stage. However, you cannot really add new square footage to the property. Therefore, focus on the size when you hunt for fix-and-flip properties.
- **Yards and gardens** – Again, most buyers would like to see a home with some open space in the form of gardens and yards. You can beautify the space and enhance its appeal as you wish but you cannot add empty space. Therefore, look for properties with this kind of open space.
- **After Repair Value (ARV)** - The ARV is the estimate of the value of a property after all the repairs, renovations, and rehabilitation works are completed. The ARV will give you a good

idea on whether the investment is worth your while or not. To get an accurate idea of the ARV of a property, you need to do the following:

- **Analyze the comparable**
- **Calculate all expenses and costs**
- **Follow the 70% Rule**

Comparables or 'comps' as they are called in the real estate market are recently sold or listed properties that are similar to your investment. Analyze these comps to determine the ARV of your property. This will give you a realistic indication of the worth of your property after repairs and renovations.

Make a detailed listing of all the costs and expenses of the rehabilitation costs. For this, take quotes from reputed contractors. Ensure you check out the quality and deliverance of these professionals. Get estimates for all your materials and ensure you get yourself a good discount for everything. As a beginner, focusing on the budget is, perhaps, the most important aspect of real estate investment.

Once you have the ARV and the expenses and costs involved, follow the 70% rule as follows: (ARV * 0.7) – Rehabilitation costs and expenses. Your cost price of the property should typically not be more than the figure thrown up by this formula.

**Mistakes to avoid while investing in fix-and-flip properties** – Succeeding in the fix-and-flip market requires a bit more skill and knowledge than the buy-and-hold strategy. Here are some obvious pitfalls that you can avoid to increase your chances for success:

Do not do work for which you are not qualified or trained, especially for skilled work like electrical and plumbing.

Choosing a property that is very far away from where you live. Daily supervision of the renovation work is an essential aspect of the fix-and-flip investment strategy. If you choose a property that is very far away, then a lot of time and energy will be wasted in the travel itself jeopardizing the quality of work and the achievement of time-bound goals.

Spending more than needed for the renovations and rehabilitation works; after all, you are not going to live in the house yourself. Therefore, plan and budget for value-added renovations, and strictly adhere to your planned budget.

As you gain experience in this strategy and build your reputation in the market, you could get investment offers wherein you don't need to put in a penny of your own money in the project.

As your reputation increases in the market driven by your successes, you are likely to find investors who are willing to pay for the entire project while you only handle the operations and get a cut from the final profits. Alternately, lenders might be willing to lend the entire money to you and expect a cut from the equity on the successful sale of the property.

**Potential risks in the fix-and-flip strategy** – Investors of the fix-and-flip strategy are exposed to the following risks:

- Underestimation of rehabilitation costs
- Holding costs exceeding expectations
- Penalties for extending loan tenures

The longer the rehabilitation work takes, the higher the costs and expenses are going to go. As you will not be able to pay back loans, especially if you have borrowed at high-interest rates from hard money lenders, then your mortgage costs are going to increase too.

There are many ways to make money in the real estate market, irrespective of what kind of property you choose to invest in. This chapter is dedicated to the various investment options you must make money in the real estate market.

## BUY AND HOLD

The buy-and-hold strategy is what most novices in the real estate market start off with. In this option, you buy a piece of property, and hold it for the long term. Buying and holding it for the long term will be called so, irrespective of whether you purchase the real estate for monthly rents or for capital growth.

One of the primary reasons for the popularity of this investment strategy is that it is an accepted thing in the real estate market that the value of a property is more or less sure to double in about 7-10 years. Therefore, the buy-and-hold strategy is great for capital growth. However, while you are in possession of the home, you can also earn rental income from it.

So, summarily, the buy-and-hold investment option means you purchase a property, take the rental income as long as you choose to hold it, and then sell it for capital gains in the future.

Some buy-and-hold investors choose to take a rehabilitation loan to renovate the house which they were able to get at a cheap rate. This renovation will help in getting a better rent than before.

The buy-and-hold strategy is a perfect choice for passive real estate investors who are looking at owning the property for a long period of time to earn monthly rentals as a secondary and/or primary income. It is also a perfect strategy for people with multiple properties or landlords who are good at managing their real estate on their own. Here are some people who thrive in the real estate market using the buy-and-hold investment strategy:

**Portfolio investors** – These individuals own multiple (between 4-10) rental properties and use professional property management service providers.

**Landlords** – These people own up to 4 properties and are good at managing by themselves.

**Turnkey properties** – These people choose to buy rental properties in faraway places (away from where they live). Turnkey projects typically come with a tenant already in place, and the property is managed by professional companies.

**1031 exchange** – Many people buy property, hold it until the property value appreciates, then sell it at a higher price so that they can buy a bigger or better property. This approach helps such investors take advantage of the capital gains tax benefit referred to as 1031 exchange.

**Costs associated with buy-and-hold strategies** – Funding for the buy-and-hold strategy is generally done through the conventional mortgage route. The following expenses and costs are typical of most buy-and-hold investments:

- Costs of financing – loan origination fees, and other fees charged by the lender
- Closing costs – typically ranges between 25 and 5%
- Maintenance costs – towards maintenance and upkeep of the said property
- Utility payments – maintenance and upkeep of the common areas associated with the property
- Property taxes
- Insurance premiums
- HOA fees (if any)

**Risks of the buy-and-hold strategy** – The primary risks associated with this kind of investment strategy are low occupancy rates and potential depreciation of property prices. Low occupancy rates can be countered by pricing your rents to cover the vacancy periods.

Price depreciation may not directly be in your control. However, you can have control over this element too by researching and choosing properties in neighborhoods that have a potential for growth. Let us look at some of the risks connected with the buy-and-hold real estate investment strategy:

**Occupancy risk** – Rental properties are not always filled by tenants. They tend to remain vacant between tenants during which time you will not be earning any rent. Additionally, you could have tenants who maintain your property poorly resulting in reduced ROI as you will have to spend more money on repair and maintenancc.

**Price depreciation** – It is possible for a property to lose value over time resulting in its price becoming less than the mortgage amount which means the investor owes more money than the worth of the property. This situation is referred to as 'the investor is underwater.'

**Defaulting on the loan** – Monthly amortization payments can sometimes become such a huge burden for buy-and-hold investors that they end up defaulting, and even becoming delinquent, on the payments. Such unfortunate situations can potentially lead to foreclosure or even bankruptcy, either of which can hurt your credibility significantly.

Personal defaults usually happen when an overenthusiastic investor borrows more money than he or she can pay back or when portfolio investors invest in more properties than they can handle at once. If you are prudent with your real estate investments, personal default can rarely occur.

**Liability risk** – Any on-site injuries caused by lack of or insufficient repair and maintenance or negligence can come to haunt portfolio investors and landlords. These investors invariably insure themselves with landlord liability insurance.

## VACATION RENTALS

Vacation rental properties are homes or houses that are typically bought in tourist destinations. These properties (comparable to Airbnb properties) can serve as a holiday home for you as the investor, and when you are not using it, you can rent the place out to visitors and tourists. For beginners, this might be a great investment option because it gives you the flexibility of using it for yourself as well as renting it out when you don't need it. The vacation rental route is good for:

- People looking for supplemental income.
- People who want to avail of rental tax benefits.

- Beginners because it is one of the simplest ways of getting your foot into the real estate investment market.
- For people who have a favorite place to travel to every year and would like to own a home there with the double benefit of offsetting vacation expenses with homeownership.

**Advantages of taking the vacation rentals investment route** – Many beginners find the idea of investing in real estate a bit daunting. For such people, vacation rentals could be a great first-step because of the following advantages:

- **Dual-purpose property** – Clearly, for a new investor, this is a great advantage. You can use this place as a second home when you are on vacation to your favorite place and rent it out when you are not using it.
- **Rental income and appreciation** – In addition to earning rental income, your property invariably appreciates in value over time, like most other real estate investments.
- **Less risky as compared to other real estate investments** – The reasons for reduced risks with vacation rentals include:
    - **Tourist destinations typically have demand for accommodation, and therefore, you have reduced vacancy risks.**

- **Rates are calculated per night-stay thereby letting you earn more faster than with traditional rental income homes.**

- **It helps you gain hands-on experience with real estate investing** – Vacation rentals allow you to be a real estate without being excessively worried about property management, especially if you use the services of vacation rental professionals. Yet, you get first-hand experience on what goes into real estate investments.

You can reduce the risk even further by choosing homes in high-demand tourist destinations. Alternately, you can choose a property that works well as vacation rentals and traditional rental income generators. So, during low occupancy times, you can rent it out as traditional homes. Therefore, when you choose your property wisely, you can switch between being a traditional landlord and an owner of a vacation rental home.

In the worst-case scenario of both these rental options failing (which happens very rarely), you always have the choice of saving money on your holidays by visiting your vacation rental place.

**Costs of purchasing vacation rental properties** – The following items are typical costs associated with investing in vacation rental properties:

- Lender fees and charges

- Closing costs associated with the mortgage
- Property taxes and insurance
- Cleaning, repairs, and maintenance
- Property management costs

Typically, vacation rental properties bring in higher rents than buy-and-hold properties considering the increased demand for accommodation in tourist places, especially during peak seasons. However, other costs such as regular cleaning and maintenance and insurance are higher too, and the increased rents offset these enhanced costs.

**Risks associated with vacation rental properties** – These are some of the potential risks you might be exposed to when you choose to invest in vacation rentals:

- Cash flows are typically inconsistent as tenants are seasonal. However, costs such as insurance, taxes, maintenances, etc. are consistent, and you are obliged to pay them irrespective of having or not having tenants. Therefore, you run the risk of being out-of-pocket.
- Vacation rentals are the first set of properties to be negatively impacted during economic downturns.

## REAL ESTATE INVESTMENT TRUSTS (REITS)

REITs are companies and trusts that either finance, operate, or own income-producing real estate. REITs operate the same way as mutual funds and offer investors to get into the real estate market at low threshold amounts. REITs provide total returns as well as dividend incomes for investors.

As an investor, you can invest in a large portfolio of real estate properties by purchasing stocks, MF units, or through exchange-traded funds (ETFs). The investor earns a share of the income proportional to his or her stock holding. With REITs, you don't need to go out, look up properties, choose what is best for you, etc. Simply invest in the REIT and obtain returns in the form of dividend income and capital appreciation in proportion to the number of stocks or units you hold.

The companies underlying the REITs lease or invest in real estate property, and the income earned from these investments are shared amongst the shareholders and unitholders in the form of dividend income. REITs are mandated to pay out at least 90% of the income earned to shareholders.

**How do REITs work?** – REITs pay their shareholders from the income they make from real estate investments. A company needs to satisfy the following elements to qualify as a REIT in addition to the other criteria needed to qualify as a trust or company:

**Different categories of REITs** – There are many categories of REITs including:

- **Equity REITs** – Most of the REITs are equity REITs, and just like mutual funds, they invest the pool of money collected from investors in income-producing real estate and share the bulk of the profits (after deducting expenses) as dividends among the shareholders. Primarily, when people mention REITs, they mean equity REITs. Equity REITs are traded on national stock exchanges.
- **Mortgage REITs** – Referred to as mREITs in short, mortgage REITs investing in real estate by creating or purchasing mortgages or by investing in mortgage-based securities. The interest income earned from these mortgages are shared amongst the shareholders.
- **Public Non-Listed REITs** – Referred to as PNLRs, the REITs of this category are registered with the Securities and Exchange Commission (SEC) but are not traded on the national stock exchanges. Investments in PNLRs typically a lock-in period and liquidity and redemption are restricted, unlike equity REITs.
- **Private REITs** – These REITs are not required to be registered with the SEC. They are, of course, not traded on national stock exchanges. Private REITs are generally bought and traded only by institutional investors.

**Advantages of investing in REITs** – Here are some of the top benefits of investing in REITs:

- **Higher dividends** – REITs are mandated to pay out at least 90% of their profits to investors resulting in higher dividend yields.
- **Professionally managed** – REITs are run and managed by experienced professionals in the real estate market ensuring your investors are in the hands of a qualified and robust team of experts. As an individual investor, you might not have the same level of capability to manage high-income-yielding large real estate properties.
- **Relatively secured and sustained income** – REITs own or manage long-term leases on commercial, residential, and other kinds of properties which can deliver a steady stream of secured rental income for a sustained period of time.
- **Portfolio diversification** – Real estate and stock markets are generally independent to each other, and they move in opposite directions. Investing in REITs enhances the power of diversification in your overall investment portfolio leading to reduced risks.
- **Transparency** – REITs are required to be registered with SECs and are subject to regulatory disclosures and other requirements which make these investment companies very transparent.

**Disadvantages of investing in REITs** – Here are some challenges and disadvantages of investing in REITs:

- **Pace of growth is slow** – REITs are allowed to reinvest only 10% of their earnings into their real estate businesses because the rest of the money has to be shared amongst the investors. Therefore, most REITs grow at slower paces than other companies.
- **Cyclical business of real estate enhances income and stability risks** – Income from real estate is cyclical resulting in an inconsistent flow of rental and other forms of income. Downturns in the real estate market could impact the stability of REITs.
- **Income from REITs are taxed differently** – REITs do not have to pay taxes on profits as 90% of their income is divided amongst investors. However, as an investor, you are required to pay taxes on dividend income from REITs by including it in your personal taxable income. It is not treated as a capital gain. So, if you belong to the higher tax bracket, you end up paying more taxes than if you had invested the money directly in real estate properties.

## CROWDFUNDING INVESTMENT OPTIONS

Crowdfunding is a new tool wherein real estate businesses raise money for their ventures by leveraging the power of social media platforms such as LinkedIn,

Twitter, and Facebook to reach out to an increased number of private individual investors.

Crowdfunding is based on the concept that many people are willing to invest small amounts of money for building a big corpus to be used for development of real estate projects. This approach is a win-win for both investors and real estate businesses. Companies can access investors who were hitherto inaccessible to them, and small-time investors have the opportunity to include real estate elements in their overall investment portfolio.

There are certain rules and regulations to be followed in the crowdfunding segment. For example, investors are screened and classified to check if they are qualified to make investments in the real estate market. Here are some ideas on what to look for and what to know about real estate crowdfunding:

**Avoid investing your retirement nest in this space** – Although real estate crowdfunding options promise high returns (and some have delivered on their promises), the high-risk-high-reward element in this space is not for your retirement funds. Keep that in capital-protected financial instruments.

**Be patient and ready yourself to wait for a long time before you reap the benefits** – Experts opine that you must be ready to wait anywhere between 5 and 7 years to begin to see liquidity and visible growth in your investments. So, be prepared for the long haul.

However, there are options wherein you can start earning money within a month of investing in a real estate crowdfunding project. Some companies need quick capital to fulfill last-leg pending orders which means returns on your investment can start sooner than later. You need to do a lot of research to find the right company for your crowdfunding entry into real estate investments.

**Look closely at the costs and the expected revenue that the company is promising** – If the company is promising something that is too good to be true, then it is time to avoid it. Look for reasonable and sustainable promises that are possible to be delivered. Don't get carried away by offerings of the moon because most scammers build their scamming business on investor naivete.

The company should offer detailed proposals that cover all aspects of the business including potential risks and how it plans to mitigate the risks. Additionally, a good company will include residual risks of their plans as well to let investors know that risks are always part of any business venture. When you see this, you feel confident you are dealing with upright people for whom integrity comes above everything else; a key element for sustained success in the business world.

**Look for company reviews** – See what earlier investors say about this venture. Are they happy or dissatisfied? Read as many reviews as you can and see what people have to say. Some of the reviews could be biased, so you must learn how to discern between genuine and fake reviews. You can also check the company's track record and see how they have fared in their earlier projects.

# CHAPTER 7: OFFERING DEALS THAT ARE IRREFUSABLE

As an investor, you want to get the best return on your investment. As such, it is crucial to identify which are the most profitable tax liens available. In recent years, there has been growing interest in tax lien investing, and for very good reasons. For starters, you can expect to receive very good rates for your investment, and also because there is very little risk involved.

If you are informed about how the process works and all other procedures, this will enable you to avoid making mistakes or costly errors. A property with a lien placed on it cannot be sold or re-financed until all taxes owed are repaid and the lien removed. As an investor, you want to find the most profitable liens in the market. Reports indicate there are over $14 billion in unpaid property taxes across the US, and about 30% of this amount is usually sold off to investors like you.

Local authorities prefer selling tax lien certificates as these bring in instant cash, which they then use to provide services to residents and execute their other obligations. Before investing your funds in a tax lien, you should choose the best strategy that fits your investment aims.

Strategies

There are several strategies that you can choose from. These include the Buy-and-Hold Strategy, Foreclosure Strategy, and Assignment Strategy. The Buy-and-Hold Strategy is best applied in states that offer the best interest rates. The Assignment Strategy is suitable for investors who wish to enter and exit a trade quickly without their money being held for lengthy periods of time, while Foreclosure Strategy will see a property sold off.

## 1. BUY-AND-HOLD STRATEGY

This strategy is best applied in states offering some of the highest interest rates in the market. You can adapt this strategy if you intend to invest in such counties, so that the interest accumulates over time. Ideally, investors often hold onto the tax lien until a property owner pays off all back taxes, or until foreclosure. For instance, the state of Florida offers interest rates of 18% on tax liens. If you invest $1,000 in tax liens for 5 years, you will earn a total of $900 in interest only.

## 2. THE ASSIGNMENT STRATEGY

This is a strategy that is preferred by investors who wish to invest in tax liens but do not want their money locked up for lengthy periods of time. You will find that most counties actually allow you to sell or transfer your liens to other investors, and sometimes even to the secondary markets. As an investor, you can also sell your tax liens at other platforms, which include online marketplaces such as eBay and others. The process is really easy as it has been digitalized for purposes of convenience.

## 3. THE FORECLOSURE STRATEGY

This is a tax lien strategy that requires you to buy a property tax lien in a given county. There is usually a certain time period that has to elapse before a property can be foreclosed. For instance, in Arizona, this period is approximately 3 years, while in Florida, this process is almost imminent.

If you intend to foreclose a property, you will need to check with the tax collector's office in the respective county. The office will notify you when the process is imminent. Once the foreclosure process is complete, you will receive the deed to the property.

## IDENTIFYING PROFITABLE TAX LIENS

Most states list their liens on their websites. As such, you should take the time to view the websites of different states across the US. Some of the more popular ones include Illinois, Florida, and Arizona. As it is right now, Florida happens to be among the most popular states, offering interest rates as high as 18% on tax liens. In fact, since this interest is not annualized, it can sometimes be as high as 36% per annum.

A rate of 36% is extremely attractive even without any penalties, and with penalties, you can expect to earn a really attractive income. Let's take the example of an investor who takes out a tax lien on a property in Florida at the rate of 18%. The lien is then redeemed seven months later, so you can collect your earnings and premium.

When you collect your return, you will actually receive a return of close to 62%, which is much better than an annualized return. Sometimes, there is a challenge to investors because the liens in some counties are not posted online. As such, your physical presence will be required at auctions. You will have to drive there and actually participate in the bids. Also, competition is often intense because of the attractive interest rates.

## PROCEDURE

You should first contact the tax office or registrar's office in any county, city, or municipality that you think has attractive liens. It is advisable to do some due diligence first.

### Due diligence

As an investor, the first thing you need to do is due diligence on the available properties. The reason is that, in some instances, the current value of a home can be much lower than the lien. As an investor, it is advisable to assess the worth of a lien certificate by dividing the amount of the delinquent tax lien with the property's market value. This ratio should not be above 4%. If it is, then you should avoid it. Some properties sometimes have more than one lien placed on them.

Each county places a distinct number on every piece of real estate with a tax lien. It is much easier for investors to search for liens using the assigned numbers. It is easy to do this online from the comfort of your home or office computer. Each number will provide you with details about a property, including their address, the property's assessed value, and the name of the owner. It will also contain information about the property's condition, as well as any other structures within the compound.

### Pay lien amount in cash

Upon purchase of a tax lien certificate, the county or municipality will expect you to pay the lien amount in full immediately. In most American states, the issuer often collects the interest amount, principal amount, and any other fees or charges. Then, he or she pays the lien certificate investor before collecting the certificate. Interest rates on liens range from 5% to almost 40%. Sometimes, investors pay a premium for the tax lien certificates. This amount is sometimes refunded, though not always.

While you are likely to receive a substantial interest rate on your investment, you really should do your homework before investing in this venture. Good understanding of the real estate market is advisable, so do your homework well before investing.

Your due diligence should include thorough research, official searches and so much more. It is actually a costly affair and can take a long while. You will need to be familiar with a property if you are to invest in a lien confidently. This will ensure that you are able to collect your money from the owner when the time comes. Also, some properties that are dilapidated or located in a tough neighborhood are not a good investment. But, you may not know this without proper due diligence.

There are properties that have suffered from some damage due to natural or environmental reasons. For instance, homes can be damaged by hazardous or chemical materials deposited in the area. Such properties are generally undesirable, and probably unsuitable for tax lien certificate investing.

Upon receiving a lien certificate, you should know what your responsibilities are. For instance, you will need to notify the property owner about the lien certificate purchase in writing. And then towards the end of the redemption period, you will need to send another reminder should payments not be received on time and in full.

Tax liens have expiration dates and do not last forever. The expiration date comes after the expiry of the redemption period. You will need to collect any unpaid monies or take some other form of action before the expiry date—otherwise, you will be unable to do so afterward. Also, should the property go into foreclosure, there is a possibility of other liens on the same property being revealed. This will likely make it difficult to acquire the title.

Large investors like hedge funds and banks have expressed an interest in tax lien investing. Such investors are able to outbid individual investors. They also drive down bids and reduce profitability. This has made it difficult for individual investors to invest profitably in tax lien certificates. Fortunately, though, there are some funds that now invest in tax lien certificates, and this opens the door for novice investors to venture into this sector.

## Repayment schedules

Tax lien certificates have repayment schedules that range from 6 months to almost 3 years. Most property owners often pay lien and charges in full. However, if they are unable to do so within the stipulated period of time, you may be required to foreclose the property even though this rarely is the case.

## Check the listings

Contact the local county's tax records or registrar's office, then request for all the tax lien listings available. You should also request for information on any impending auctions. These are usually available, and you will only pay the cost of printing. You can do this across a number of counties in several states. It is at this stage that you will do your due diligence.

Once you have done your due diligence, you will then proceed to select the properties that you are interested in. You should contact the relevant office and confirm a couple of things, such as the interest rates that the county will pay for the taxes owed. Sometimes, this percentage is high even though it varies from state to state. As soon as you identify a lien that you are interested in, you should proceed to the tax office and pay for the lien. Do so in cash if you can, and you will be registered as the holder of the lien of the particular home.

Make sure that you receive the tax lien certificate complete with dates and a payment receipt. You should keep these documents handy until such a time when the lien expires, or when the homeowner finally pays his or her dues. This is why securely keeping your documents is crucial. Once the property's back taxes are completely paid off, you will then proceed to collect all your dues. Your final payment will include your initial investments, all interests accruing, as well as any penalties due.

Should the homeowner fail to pay their property taxes on time and the tax lien expires, then you will have to seize the property immediately. The law requires that the liens and interests have to be paid in full before, or at the expiration of the lien. If not, then the property legally becomes yours. You will be at liberty to begin the eviction process, and the local sheriff's office will be able to assist here.

You can also attend tax lien auctions, which can happen across some states. In these states, the authorities often seize and auction properties where liens have expired, unpaid. These are often conducted by the county's tax office or sometimes even the sheriff's department. If you attend an auction, then you will be required to pay a certain amount of money. You will also be expected, if you place a winning bid, to pay at least 10% of the total amount, and the remaining amount within a period of

10 to 30 days. If you acquire a home through an auction or lien, renovate it and then sell it off for a profit. There are plenty of willing buyers out there looking for a good deal, so you will very likely find a buyer for the property.

# CHAPTER 8: FLIPPING YOUR REAL ESTATE

The fix-and-flip investment strategy is for short-term investors who can identify and pick up property that is in poor shape, fix it, and then sell it for a much higher price than the cost for profits. Typically, such investors want to complete the entire cycle of buying, fixing, and selling properties within a span of 12 months.

The fix-and-flip strategy is ideal for brokers, contractors, and realtors who have plenty of experience in the real estate market. Additionally, experienced rehabbers use this strategy to build wealth. Ideally, the fix-and-flip investment strategy is best for rehabbers who have some amount of experience in rehabilitation. However, in today's real estate markets, you can find professional rehabilitation agents who can take up the contract even for novice real estate investors.

Here are some useful tips on how to make the fix-and-flip strategy make money for you:

**First, create a concrete flipping plan** – You must have a clear, goal-oriented, and time-bound business plan to succeed in the fix-and-flip investment strategy. This plan not only gives you a clear pathway for progress with well-defined milestones, but it will also boost lender confidence in your capability and commitment in finishing the project successfully. Your flipping plan should have the following elements:

- Specific and time-bound goals including details of how you plan to achieve them
- Types of properties you plan to target along with reasons for your choice
- Location of the property
- Who is going to do the rehabilitation work? A paid contractor or you yourself? Reasons and separate plans have to be enclosed for this too
- Timeline of the entire project, which should typically be 90 days, and definitely not more than 12 months
- Marketing/advertising plan to sell the renovated house
- If you are planning to make a business out of this investment strategy, then set up your business as well
- Expected ROI with concrete evidence from experts such as expected market value of the property after renovation, the growth prospects in the chosen location, etc.

**Choose the right professionals in the market** – You will need expert professionals such as lawyers, realtors, rehabilitation contractors, accountants, and others to make a success of your fix-and-flip investment. Choose your professionals wisely. Connect with many people, speak to them, learn about what they do, read their reviews, and do your homework before deciding on which expert you are going to go with.

**Find lenders for your investment plans** – If you don't have hard cash for the fix-and-flip investment, then you need to find sound lenders for your project(s). There are primarily three types of lenders who can finance your flipping project(s).

- **Hard money loans** – You can find plenty of private investors and/or companies who lend money against property security. The approval and processing times are much faster than traditional mortgages. Hard money lenders are more lenient than traditional lenders. However, their interest rates are steeper than the market rates and their loan terms are all for short-term only.
- **Rehabilitation loans** – Some lenders extend credit lines on existing mortgages which can be used to rehabilitate another project.

**Investment group loans** – When you join real estate investor groups, you are likely to find interesting private individuals or groups of people who are willing to lend you money for your rehabilitation project. These kinds of lenders are likely to bet their money on people with successful experience in the fix-and-flip investment market.

# CHAPTER 9: GETTING CASH FLOW FROM YOUR PROPERTY

In this section we want to talk about the financials that you need to consider when dealing with a tenant buyer. I am talking about financials at the start of the transaction, financials through the term of the deal and the financials required to close the deal. This is not to be confused with the ways you will make money with Lease Options.

In this section, wc arc going to look at the decisions you have to make regarding all of financials related to a Lease Option. How you are going to treat all that money? How much money are you going to collect from the tenant? How you are going to apply those funds? How are you going to approve that tenant based on the financing they have to get at the end of the deal?

The first financial component is the upfront deposit. There's a few things that you have to consider when you are looking at the deposit. First of all, is it a deposit or an option credit or an option consideration or a down payment? All these terms mean basically the same thing. However, you also need to be aware of how these deals would be viewed by the banks. There are a few issues that you might run into depending on how you treat that upfront deposit.

The next financial component happens throughout the length of the Lease Option arrangement. These financial items are the monthly credits and the monthly profits.

Profit is not really a tenant consideration even though the tenant is paying for the profit.

During the term of the Lease Option program, there is an amount that you may have added to the monthly payment that may be credited towards their purchase, should the tenant decide to buy. Obviously, when considering adding this credit to the tenant's lease payment, you have to make sure that it's something the tenants can afford. You want to make sure that the total payment isn't so high that the tenants are going to be moving out in 6 months because they just keep paying that amount.

The base monthly payment is set so that is covers all the housing costs. There's also the credit component that will be added that you will be crediting the tenant when they purchase the property. And, finally, the other monthly component is the profit. The monthly profit is an additional amount that you might add to provide a reasonable overall profit for the deal. You may want to add this monthly profit because the back end price is so low due to low appreciation in that area.

The third financial component that you need to be concerned with is the down payment the tenant has to save for. When it comes time for the tenant to buy the property, they are buying it for an already agreed to price. They will be using the initial deposit and the monthly credits as the down payment.

The down payment that you might be helping the tenant save for is 5% of the purchase price. However, you might want to consider helping them save for 10%. This would allow for some money for the closing costs which can be anywhere form 2% to 4% of the purchase price.

You want to make sure that all the contracts are structured so that when the tenant goes to purchase the property, they have enough money available to complete the transaction. You will have to help the tenant out with all that planning and preparation and the accumulation of the down payment for the eventual purchase and closing.

## TENANT DEPOSIT

The first tenant buyer financial item that you need to be concerned with is the deposit.

The deposit, or the option consideration as it is sometimes referred to, is the amount of money that the tenant is going to put down to be able to move into a particular property. The option consideration gives the tenant the right to purchase this property at some time in the future for an agreed to price.

For example, if we have a property worth $300,000 and the future price is $330,000, a 5% down payment would require that the tenant saves $16,500. The initial deposit that they pay, let's say it's $10,000, would go towards that down payment for the eventual purchase of that house.

There are a few things to take into consideration when determining the amount of the deposit / option fee to ask for.

The first thing is the income of the tenant. The second thing is your comfort level with an individual or the risk tolerance against the individual. And the third thing is the price of the home.

If that tenant is only making $20,000 a year and are trying to purchase a property for $300,000 and they can only put down $2,000, that's not going to work. The minimum deposit that I ask for in my area is $10,000. But sometimes there's exceptions. Sometimes I would allow a smaller deposit amount depending on the credit capability of a person and their income. Then I would in place a payment program to collect the balance.

So for example I have one gentleman right now and his credit score is 720, which is a very good credit score. He has 2 incomes. One as an employee and the other as a side business. However, the banks won't recognize his side business. But through the due diligence that we have done, we know that he makes twice as much as what the banks thinks he makes. So what we did is we have a Lease Option arrangement where he is paying $2,000 a month for his Lease Option payment. He only put down a small deposit of $2,000 but we are collecting another $1,000 a month for his deposit. So because of his income we negotiated a lower initial deposit.

You really want a minimum deposit of $10,000, unless you have exceptions like I just mentioned. But the deposit amount could also depend on the price of the house.

For example, another deal I have is that I have a person in a property that we paid almost $500,000 for. This is a very expensive Lease Option agreement for my area. Now I only asked him to put down $10,000. Between him and his wife, they make about $200,000 a year. So they have the income to support it but at the same time I'm very concerned that he doesn't have enough equity in the deal and he has missed a few payments.

We are now coming time to close the deal and I don't think his credit is good enough to qualify. I am concerned that he may walk away from the deal since he has $10,000 into the deal and he could walk away. Now he does have about $26,000 in credits that he has accumulated over the last 3 years, but I am still concerned that we may have to sell and not get our money out of this deal.

For high-end homes, I should have probably asked for a $20,000 deposit or maybe even a $25,000 deposit. A rule of thumb that some investors use when determining the amount of deposit to ask for, is that they want a minimum of 5% down from the tenant buyer.

Some people think that if they had 5% to put down, they wouldn't need us. And sometimes that's the case. But to qualify for a mortgage, lenders will look at the income of the applicant, the down payment they have, and their credit score. Obviously, it's not just how much down payment they have. So make sure you explain that to your prospective client.

One important point to make is that, it's better to have an empty unit than a bad tenant.

If you put somebody in a property and they have only given a deposit of $1,000, or even worse only $500, and they are paying $500 a month to accumulate that down payment, there's not a lot of "skin in the game" so to speak. My experience has been that most of those people are not a good risk.

When I was just starting my Lease Option business, I had a lot of tenant buyer's default on me because I allowed them to enter into an arrangement without a high enough deposit. Again, that minimum may be lower for certain towns.

For example, one town that I invest in you can purchase a home for $100,000. In that town I might allow a minimum of only $5,000 for the deposit. In other towns where my homes are worth $300,000, I require a minimum of $10,000.

## TENANT MONTHLY PAYMENTS

The next tenant financial component that we will look at is the monthly payment.

The monthly payment is the lease payment that the tenant has to pay monthly. When setting the lease payment amount, you want to make sure it covers a number of things.

## MONTHLY COSTS

The first thing is you want to ensure that the monthly payment covers all your monthly costs. Your monthly costs include the mortgage principal, interest, taxes and insurance (PITI). Those are all the normal costs associated with owning a home.

At a minimum, the monthly lease payment that the tenant is paying has to cover those costs. You never want to be out of pocket. You never want to have a negative cash flow when doing these deals. I've heard some investors say that they can't find any good deals so they are taking a negative cash flow and they will make it up in the back end when they sell. This is the wrong approach. There's all kinds of ways to make sure that you have a positive cash flow in these arrangements.

## MONTHLY CREDIT

The second component that makes up the monthly payment is the monthly credit. The monthly credit is an amount that you add to the monthly payment that will eventually go towards the tenants' down payment when they buy. This is a form of forced savings for the tenant buyer.

Let's say, for example, the tenant buyer needs a down payment of $20,000 to purchase the home. They give an initial deposit of $10,000. This means they have to save an additional $10,000. This would require an additional monthly credit payment of approximately $300 a month spread over 36 months, if you are using a 3-year term.

What you would do in this case is add that $300 to their monthly payment. This accumulated credit will be applied to the down payment when they purchase.

Never allow the tenant to save this amount on their own and not pay you the monthly credit payment. First of all, you want to make sure that that credit amount is paid to you since it also provides you with cash flow. Secondly, the tenant hasn't been able to save for their down payment up until now, so don’t leave it up to them to save for the balance. You have to make sure the money is there when it comes time to close in 3 years. Sure they might have been able to save the initial $10,000 for the deposit but now that they are paying a higher monthly lease payment and all their other expenses. It might be more difficult for them to save.

So you want to make sure that you are collecting ALL the money that will be used for the down payment when it comes time to purchase. Don't leave anything to chance.

## MONTHLY PROFIT

The third component of the monthly payment is profit. Some people think you can't add an additional amount to the monthly payment, other than what is required to cover your costs. Sure you can. You are trying to make a certain return on these investments. Some investors are charging a lot of profit to the point where it's outrageous. I'm not suggesting that you do that.

Your overall profit is based on the eventual sale of the property. The sale price was based on the estimated appreciation. But it may be that you are concerned about where the economy is and what the property would actually be worth at the end of the lease purchase agreement. One of the things you can do is reduce the sale price and increase the monthly payments to include a profit amount. This would allow you to continue to make the profit you want while keeping the back end sale price within reason. For example, you could add $200 or $300 or $400 to the monthly payment and decrease the eventual sale price of the property to the tenant buyer.

If you decide that you are going to increase the monthly payment this way and decrease the eventual purchase price, you have to make sure the tenant can afford to make this higher monthly payment. You need to evaluate a tenant using the standard banks evaluation process.

When evaluating a tenant's financial capability, I use the standard gross debt service (GDS) and total debt service (TDS) ratios. When using the GDS, I don't allow their total house payment to exceed 32% of their gross incomes. So if their lease payment is $2,000 a month, they have to make approximately $6,000 per month or $72,000 per year. That's the minimum income they need to be earning.

I also look at their TDS and won't approve anyone whose TDS is greater than 40%. So if the applicants have car payments, credit card payments, etc. totaling $1,500 and their lease payment is $2,000, they would have a monthly payment of $3,500. This means the minimum income required is $8,750 per month or $105,000 per year ($105,000*40%/12)

## TENANT DOWN PAYMENT

The last financial component that you need to be concerned with is the tenant's down payment. What I am referring to here is not the upfront deposit payment but rather the down payment the tenant needs to accumulate for their eventual purchase.

The key to the down payment is that you have to make sure that the tenants have accumulated a large enough down payment so that they can purchase the property. This down payment is calculated based on the purchase price.

For example, let's say the purchase price is $300,000 and the tenant has to accumulate 5% for the down payment, which is $15,000. Assuming they gave you a $10,000 upfront deposit, then you have to collect another $5,000 over the length of the contract.

This down payment that the tenant is saving, is the down payment that they are going to use to purchase the property. Sometimes they think that these accumulations of deposits and credits are refundable.

They think that, if they don't buy the property they get their money back. In my transactions, if they do not buy the property, then they do not get their money back.

The amount of money that the tenant contributed to their down payment, through the initial deposit and the monthly credits, are not refundable. Make sure that they know this. Make sure that there is a waiver or statement that you get them to sign upfront, stating that it is non-refundable.

In fact, your tenants may decide that they aren't going to purchase the property. By doing so, they walk away and waive their right to their initial deposit and their monthly credits.

For example, I had one couple that put down $20,000 and moved into the property. A few months later, they decided they didn't want the property. They moved out and didn't notify us. They tried to get their deposit back by getting their lawyer to come after us. But they lost since the contracts were clear that the deposit was non-refundable.

The down payment, that the tenants are accumulating, has to be an amount that the bank would accept.

For example, I mentioned 5% is in an amount that most banks require. But maybe the tenants are self-employed and maybe the bank that you are dealing with or the banks in your area require 10% or 20% from a self-employed individual.

You have to take this into consideration when determining how much of a down payment the tenant should be saving for. Especially in today's market, where it is harder for people to get qualified for a mortgage.

The other thing you may want to consider is that you may want the tenant to save additional money for the closing costs.

Closing costs could be as high as 2%. So it may be that you want the tenant to save 7%. 2% of that can be used for closing costs and 5% for the down payment.

Remember, you have to make sure you are evaluating the tenant's credit along the way, using a good credit management program. You want to make sure that they are ready to purchase when we need them to purchase.

You also have to keep good records of the deposit and of the credits that have been paid.

For example, when the tenants write you a check for the $10,000 deposit, make sure that they keep the statement or that they get their bank statement that shows they wrote a check for $10,000. Maybe even take a picture of that check and keep it on file. You also want to keep track of the monthly payments.

There has to be a clear way to show the lender that the down payment has been collected from the tenant throughout the program.

# CHAPTER 10: INTRODUCTION TO COMMERCIAL REAL ESTATE

A successful partnership is one of the best ways to enter the world of commercial real estate. In short, you need to network, meet, mingle, and know others for the simple purpose of creating mutual support or assistance towards moving one another forward.

Networking does not need to be a formal or methodical activity. Instead, your daily interactions with people should be integral to your networking strategy. Let networking be your lifestyle, your way of life!

The real estate industry, as always, has its own share of the good times and the bad times—the equally interesting rise and fall of fortunes. Back in 2006, just before the housing financial crisis, the membership of the National Association of Realtors (NAR) hit an all-time record high of a little below 1.5 million.

During and after the bursting of the housing bubble, however, it nosedived dramatically to its rock bottom of less than a million members in 2012. A rejuvenated membership had only picked up the slack a couple of years later; and since then, it has kept on increasing steadily, reaching 1.3 million members as of 2017.

Indeed, the current competition is becoming fiercer than ever. Nowadays, you ought to step up your efforts to survive and thrive, especially amidst the changing times and the fast-paced advancements in technological innovations.

Essentially, commercial real estate increases the risks relative to residential investments. Commercial properties are larger, require more funding, and require more accountability.

## REAL ESTATE PARTNERSHIP TAXATION

One other point against building a new property is that none of these costs are tax-deductible. You are on the hook for all payments related to this property and the interest on the mortgage is not tax deductible.

Consequently, building a rental property is simply not worth it. Turn-key properties will enable you to rent them quickly with minimal costs associated with its maintenance or repairs. Ideally, you'd be looking at places you wouldn't actually be living in. And if you are keen on short-term rentals, you can put some serious money in your pocket and get a couple of tax breaks on top.

In the final section of this chapter, we will be taking a closer look at the risks involved in owning a rental property.

## PROS AND CONS OF REAL ESTATE PARTNERSHIPS

A real estate partnership is a nice idea for anyone who may have gaps in their knowledge or experience in real estate. On the other hand, a truly excellent partnership can easily be the only thing new investors require to get off to a great start. Here are some of the many benefits of real estate partnerships:

- **The right partner can bring additional resources to the table, including capital or a wide area network.**
- **A real estate partnership structure offers both parties more flexibility in the distribution of profits and losses.**
- **Partners can bring another perspective when analyzing agreements and possible investments.**
- **The combined real estate partner portfolios can help bring the wow factor to meetings with potential lenders.**
- **Partnerships are about balance, allowing both parties to share and**

**assume their responsibilities and workload.**

Basically, a good partner can bring something to the table that you may not have at the moment, be it access to capital or market experience in your preferred investment area. That said, partnerships are not for everyone. Consider the following disadvantages associated with real estate investment partners:

- **Revenues must be distributed among the partners, which degrades profits.**
- **Real estate partners may possess very different management styles, which can lead to organizational conflicts.**
- **If the partnership agreement is not totally clear, it can be difficult to delegate responsibilities (or losses).**
- **Partnerships can make unnecessary efforts to create a healthy friendship.**
- **In some cases, a partner can bring more to the table, creating a disparity in terms of equity or skills.**

## STRUCTURING A REAL ESTATE INVESTMENT PARTNERSHIP

How investors structure a real estate partnership can lead directly to its success or failure. Therefore, this part of the process should not be taken lightly by a trading partner.

### Find the right partner

If nothing else, a partner should be in charge of bringing something new to the table. And while it's perfectly acceptable for your potential partner to share some of the unique skills you've already exposed, he should offer a free skill set. In other words, the partner with whom you decide to align must fill a distinct void and meet a specific need. Only by adding a free skill set will your business become more versatile and better prepared to handle what the real estate market holds.

### Attention to your diligence

Concluding a real estate partnership is not something you take seriously, and you should not do it without thinking of things from an objective point of view. As I said before, you need to be sure to partner for the right reasons, but it's equally vital to select the right partner. Not only must they complement your skills to maximize their utility, but they must also be a trusted person. When evaluating your potential partner, it is of the utmost importance that they can do their job well. So, you must make sure they can. You are the ultimate guardian, so make sure your partner is competent.

## Define roles and expectations

Before joining a partnership, it is in your interest to determine what is expected of each individual and the roles they will inherently assume. This will reduce the risk of experiencing significant problems later. Note that the more accurately you can define the role of each partner, the better. There should be literally no difference as to the role you will play throughout your involvement in the business. Who will manage the finances? Who will be responsible for marketing? Which of you will be responsible for negotiating at the closing table? Partners must know who is doing what well before the situation arises. In this way, you can set reasonable expectations for which each partner will be retained.

## Define the terms

Once you've decided how to delegate responsibilities, it's time to move on to a more complicated conversation: delegate profits and losses. All partnership structures of real estate investment have a contract type, which determines the exact terms of the contract for the business. A common structure will determine the number of profits allocated to the company and then the distribution of the leftovers between the partners. For example, the terms of your contract may be to maintain 40% of your company's profits and subsequently a 50/50 split between partners. There are infinite possibilities for the terms of the contract. Make sure you find some with which both parties agree.

## Keep it simple

Avoid complicating the task when you enter your partnership actual structure. You need to anticipate business ops, but you do not have to plan lunch breaks right now. Remember to stay focused when you negotiate and stay simple (but complete). At this point, it is also important not to abuse the legalese. Both partners need to understand explicitly what they are engaging in. Formality is important for the maintenance of professionalism; however, you must understand exactly what you are engaging in. Work with a real estate lawyer or legal team and use the language everyone comprehends.

## Protect yourself

Right now, you have worked to create an ideal business partnership, but this does not guarantee that you will be safe from challenges. You and your partner must engage in steps to protect yourself if something goes wrong in the future. This means setting up the right corporate structure to protect your personal assets, whether through an LLC or something else. Each of these conditions must be examined with a lawyer and entered into a binding contract. Although no one wants the worst scenario to happen, it is essential that you and your partner be protected, if at all.

## Setting goals

Do not overlook the goals and long-term aspirations of your potential partner. In fact, understanding what your partner wants from this exchange is invaluable, especially for emerging companies. If it was just nothing else, getting a clearer picture of what your partner wants from the impending partnership can make or break things in the future. That said, you must be absolutely sure that each of your goals is aligned. Partnering with someone with different intentions makes no sense. At worst, you can compromise the entire business.

# CHAPTER 11: TIPS TO MAXIMIZE PROFIT

As a wholesaler, you benefit from the price of reselling the property without becoming the sole owner.

Wholesaling is also known as flipping. It bears several advantages over other real estate businesses. You do not need an office to operate from; neither do you need employees or insurance cover for your business.

Strategies:

When it comes to real estate wholesaling, there are several strategies used to gain buyers and sellers on the market today. These strategies help you to get real estate opportunities that you can engage in to generate profit. The primary point is always to find the right deals and maximize your time on them to get something good out of them. Some of the strategies you can use to get buyers and sellers include:

- **Direct mail marketing**
- **Local marketing**
- **Networking**
- **Online marketing**
- **Driving for dollars**

## Direct Mail Marketing

When you are a wholesaler, you want to get deals at a price that is below the market price. This is what enables you to make a profit. The cost must balance in a way that ensures the buyer makes some profit should he decide to resell the property. If the price of the property is set too high, the buyer might get stuck, meaning he will not be able to sell the property off.

A great way to obtain deals that are favorably priced is through the use of direct email. To use this strategy, you need to first come up with a list of your target clients then keep emailing these severally. The good thing with direct mail is that you can acquire email lists from third parties. These lists are often customized in a way that meets your wholesaling requirements. They always contain names and contacts of homeowners who are seeking to either purchase or sell off properties. You must note, however, that getting these lists will cost you some money.

When you consistently send emails to the contacts on your list, you will be able to get some leads. The content of your message matters a lot since it will determine how your target buyers respond to your requests. You must, therefore, identify a particular motivation and incorporate it into your communications. For instance, if a seller promises to give out their property then change their mind later, you may offer some discount that will keep them in the deal. This also applies to the buyer; especially when the property in question needs some repair work done after the purchase. How you follow up on your leads also determines if you will get them. The buyer or seller may fail to contact you, but if you keep refreshing your conversations with them, you might land a great deal from them.

Most buyers who have used this strategy always admit that it is one of the best ways to create a consistent flow of real estate wholesaling opportunities. Once you have categorized potential buyers and sellers in terms of location, income level, and age among other attributes, it is easy for you to know when to send them. As your business grows, the lists may also increase significantly. At this point, you may need to engage a third party individual or organization to be sending the emails on your behalf. This is what makes direct mail a bit expensive. However, the strategy remains relevant when you are making enough profit from it. For example, you may spend $2000 on the costs of sending the emails but get three deals that give you a profit of $6000.

In this strategy, you spend money to gain money. You can therefore not use it effectively if you do not have any money allocated to it. Most wholesalers have testified of closing up to 90 percent of the deals sought using this strategy. Mailers always comprise of postcards and letters. The way you design these mails determines how they are received. Always ensure that you use a promotional tone.

## Networking

Another great strategy you may use to get deals for your business is by interacting with other real estate investors. You can achieve this by joining networking groups within your local area. You may also join some online networking forums where you can get information about real estate networking events within your area. As you continue to network with others, you may be lucky enough to find investors who are willing to delegate some deals to you. This can occur when the investor has too many transactions or is just too old to transact. You may also find wholesalers that are seeking to partner with others for one reason or the other. All this only creates more business for you.

Most estates always have at least one club created explicitly for real estate investors. If you want to get deals within your area quickly, you must join such clubs. These create an avenue for you to land some of the most excellent deals. As you build your credibility and reputation in such clubs, you will stand a high chance of succeeding in your business. You must always treat everyone you meet in such clubs with courtesy because you may not know who will eventually become your client.

Such clubs always comprise of sellers and buyers. As you interact with people, you will always find some buyers who are just seeking the right person to give their property to. You will also learn a lot from some of the experts within your local area. Joining such clubs may cost you a small amount of cash, but it is worth trying. Eventually, you will become the go-to wholesaler for most deals that arise within your area. Investors who have a lot of deals on their hands may approach you to assist them. Even if such agreements do not give you much in terms of profit, they can help you build your brand. Eventually, you will be able to get deals without having to market your business too much. Always remember that wholesaling is a relationship-based kind of investment. The more relationships you cultivate, the more profitable your business gets.

### *Local Marketing*

Local marketing entails looking for deals within your local market. This is one of the cheapest real estate wholesaling strategies. You can begin by creating some visual signs and posters. You have probably seen samples of these on telephone poles and buildings within your estate. You can create these signs and add your contact number in case someone wants to reach out to you for a deal.

One great attribute that makes these signs work is where you position them. For example, you can opt to place them at a junction, next to a mall or anywhere where there is high human traffic. When used correctly, this strategy becomes more effective than direct mail campaigns. You can also decide to buy a list of FSBO properties within your area then contact their owners to get some deals within your area. Most FSBO property owners avoid using agents because of the massive commissions involved. However, if you approach them with a better deal than that of the agents, you may convince them to give you the work of selling the property on their behalf.

### *Online Marketing*

Online platforms grant you the opportunity to reach out to millions of people within a few seconds. One such platform is social media. To use online platforms effectively, you need to set up a website where users can get more information about your wholesaling business. You can decide to set up a simple website using WordPress or a more dynamic website using more sophisticated tools.

When done creating the website, you can come up with profiles on Facebook, Instagram, Twitter, and many others, depending on your preference. Highlight your business terms and conditions on these profiles while also ensuring that you remain promotional. Make your posts on these platforms consistent. You will be able to get connections and referrals to great wholesaling opportunities. However much you desire to make a profit, ensure that you do not exaggerate your terms of business. At first, you may receive only a few or no leads, but as you continue to build your accounts, you will realize more and more opportunities coming through. Sometimes you may stay for several days or weeks without getting any deal. This should not discourage you from continuing to build your online presence.

Besides social media, you may also decide to get some deals on Craigslist. The site has a real estate section that highlights excellent wholesaling deals. One advantage of the craigslist system is that it is free to use and you can automate your deals flow with ease. It is the best alternative to direct mail marketing since you do not spend any cash on marketing your business.

### *Driving for Dollars*

The fifth and last strategy is known as driving for dollars. This strategy is commonly used by dedicated wholesalers who are ready to go to any extent to get a wholesaling deal. The approach involves driving within your areas of interest to look for properties that indicate distress. Some of the things to look for include broken walls, windows, neglected compounds, and junk in the compound.

When you spot such a house, you can write down the exact location address then visit the relevant online platforms to find out more about the property. If you get information about the owners of the property, you contact them by mail or phone to find out if they are willing to sell the property.

Most wholesalers do not like this strategy because it involves a lot of processes. However, when you become committed to it, you can easily land some good deals at no cost at all. The more you understand the area of interest, the easier it becomes for you to identify some properties in distress.

## How to Make a Profit from Wholesaling

As a wholesaler, the amount of money you make from any deal depends on many factors. Before getting into any agreement, you need first to understand the property after repair value or ARV. You have to know how much you can sell the property once it has been fully renovated.

Determining the ARV of a property entails comparing some of its aspects with other properties. This also includes comparing the price of the property with others within the area in terms of the pricing. You can do this by identifying a few properties that share some characteristics with your potential investment, then using these to carry out the comparison. This will help you to estimate the final cost of the property once you have completed all the repairs.

Understanding that wholesalers are only matchmakers that link buyers to sellers enable you to know how much you will make from a deal before closing it. One advantage of wholesaling is that you can use several ways to gain profit. How best you negotiate an agreement with the buyer and seller determines how much you earn from it when the deal closes. Remember, as a wholesaler you only make a certain percentage as wholesaling fees although some sellers may be generous enough to share part of the profit with you.

If you do not carry out your deals right, you may spend several years working with individuals who do not sell anything. You may also find yourself wholesaling for a property no one wants to purchase. The kind of strategy you use to get deals also has a way of influencing your returns. This is because strategies like bandit signs or listing on MLS can get you instant opportunities that process quickly. Other strategies like direct mail and driving for dollars can take a while before you realize any opportunities. Delayed processing of deals translates to late income.

Another factor that influences the profit you make from wholesaling is the kind of property you get. When it comes to this kind of investment, the numbers or price usually dictates the direction of the business. You must always purchase the property at a cost that is low enough to be able to resell at a profit. The buyer only gets interested in a property whose price is attractive. This may sometimes mean that you make less profit than what you had in your initial plan. It is better to make relatively little profit from several deals than making one huge profit over a stretched period.

When it comes to analyzing the profitability of a particular house, there are several computations that you need to make. One such calculation is the 70 percent rule which states that the maximum offer you can receive for a property is 70% of its value after repair. In case you do not understand how to make these computations, you should consult a professional to do it on your behalf. In case you ignore these calculations, you will end up with wrong figures. You will stand at risk of losing some cash instead of making a profit from the property. Some deals may also take a long time to process. You must factor the aspect of time in all your computations to ensure that the property does not depreciate during the process.

The next thing you need to check out when determining your profits is the market. The kind of market you list the property impacts how long the process will take and how much you will take home as wholesaling fees. Start looking for buyers early enough. Some wholesalers postpone this until when they are about to close the deal with the seller. You need always to have a list of buyers ready even before the seller commits the property to you. As you look for deals, concurrently look for buyers as this will save you time in case the seller agrees to your deal. You can get these online or through your local investment clubs. You may also use newspaper ads and other networking events to identify potential buyers. If a property receives more than one buyer, you can decide to give priority to those buyers you have dealt with previously.

The ultimate goal of making a profit lies in building strong, lasting relationships. People that are conversant with your business tend to invest in it more than strangers. Working with people you know eases the burden of convincing them to purchase or sell properties to you. When an issue arises with the property, it becomes easier to resolve since you have already gained the trust of the parties involved. Seeking to make things easy for the investors you work with makes them wish to work with you more in the future. However, if you are the person that leaves issues unresolved, then you will lose some future wholesaling opportunities to other investors in your circle.

To better understand how much you can make from a deal, you mustn't exaggerate your profits. Increasing the actual property cost just to earn more from it may land you one or two contracts. Once buyers and sellers know of this trick, they will start avoiding your business. Remember, real estate investors always interact with one another. Spoiling your reputation with one may mean destroying it for all. Therefore you must be careful about the image you create with all the investors that you work with. Get to understand the prices on the market and ensure that you do not exceed them. If you want the business to continue working in your favor, always keep all the numbers associated with a particular deal real.

There are a few tips associated with wholesaling costs and profits. These can help you remain on course when anticipating earnings from a specific property. Let us look at some of them:

1. **Choose a comfortable price range** – a good number of the deals you will come across fall in the middle range when it comes to prices. Some will even have lower rates than expected. However, you always need to set a price that is favorable to you, so long as it falls within the range recommended to the buyer and seller. If you set the prices too low, you might end up getting properties that have less demand and a lot of repair issues. This will result in less or no buyer for the property.

2. **Understand the cost of repairs** – this is a distinctive aspect of wholesaling. Majority of the properties listed for sale feature several repair issues. You must add this cost to your final value of the property. For instance, if you do not know how to estimate the price of the property ensure that you only get one that costs 70% or less than the market value. The lower the cost, the higher your profits.

3. **Identify buyers with cash** – get a buyer who has a higher potential of purchasing the property. It does not make sense, getting a buyer who is only keen to make promises but not delivering to the contract. You must verify that the buyer is serious about purchasing the property before closing out other potential buyers.

4. **Choose the right neighborhoods** – good neighborhoods are those that feature reasonably priced properties. Lower prices may be useful for you, but in most cases, such properties do not get quick buyers. You must target some areas where other real estate wholesalers are thriving. Insecurity and several other challenges often characterize some low priced neighborhoods.

Besides these four tips, you must always look for ways to process deals faster. This is because speed and volume matter a lot when it comes to wholesaling properties for profit.

Real Estate is known to be a market which is equally rich in potential as well as risk, and there is no limit when it comes to acquiring knowledge pertaining to the factors which influence it. In many cases even the most seasoned real estate agents have admitted to overlooking small but significant factors which serve to drastically impact the total value of a piece of real estate.

- Easy to comprehend examples and analyses of various investment decisions; these case studies will help first time investors in understanding the importance of identifying ideal market conditions which enable profitable investing, and methods through which one can limit their risk factors.
- Clear guidelines with regard to the step-by-step processes associated with identifying, assessing, and making investments.
- Practical advice pertaining to using leverage (primarily, Time, People, and Money) in order to maximize your net worth.
- Information which can help in helping you know when to buy and when to hold
- Valuable tips on how to organize financing
- Strategies pertaining to rehabbing; from estimating costs to organizing logistics, finding supplies, and managing expenses.
- Definitions of terminology pertaining to the Real Estate market, buying, and selling, which will enable new investors and estate agents to remove any

confusion associated with words and phrases used while discussing or defining certain processes.

Developing a clear understanding of the Real Estate market will enable readers to gain an insight into how the market functions, grows, and fluctuates. The development of this understanding will facilitate a more grounded approach towards making a smart investment decision, which is why it is important that this book be read from start to finish.

## UNDERSTANDING THE DO'S AND DON'TS OF THE REAL ESTATE MARKET

Do: Organize and understand your personal finances prior to making any investments.

One of the most important things you will need to consider prior to investing in real estate is to have your own personal property. It is important to be in possession of your own property for the simple reason that this basic security is important for your daily living needs and sustainability. It is recommended that you spend a few weeks in understanding your level of expenditure in order to gain an overall picture of your needs, savings, and most importantly, how much free cash you will have left to invest. Some things to also factor in while organizing your finances are any potential future investments which are not real estate related but will require considerable investment; this could range from a new car to building a new section within your existing house.

Do: Conduct enough research in order to find out as much as you can about your investment.

It is of primary importance for you to evaluate a potential investment prior to committing; this especially applies to an investment which looks too good to be true. Always conduct a SWOT (Strengths, Weaknesses, Opportunities, and Threats) analysis in order to effectively assess the pros and cons of the investment in question. If an investment seems too good to be true, chances are, it probably is.

Don't: Ignore your gut instinct.

Regardless of whether you are a first time investor or have a lot of experience, it is always advisable for you to trust your gut when it comes to making or not making an investment. There are situations which may seem favorable or otherwise, but your gut tells you to wait or commit; trust your inner voice, do not ignore it. Exercising due diligence in terms of research will enable you to develop your gut instinct further; you can improve it by following the previous suggestion of always conducting your own research and forming your own assessments aside from what is shared with you by realtors and agents.

Don't: Underestimate the value of good tenants and their ability to preserve your property value.

It is wise to conduct business with, i.e. rent your property out to reliable and responsible tenants who are likely to pay you on time and value your property. Finding tenants with a good credit history and stable jobs might take more time, but it will be worth it in the end since they will reside in your property longer and will be less likely to cause damage. A natural benefit to this decision would involve reduced repair and renovation costs once they move out and you are ready to sell or rent to new tenant. Never rush into a decision pertaining to renting your property; therefore, it could cost you in the long run.

Do: Understand and acknowledge the fact that the bottom line is all that is important in the end.

There are investments which look like they would be ideal for your budget, but are actually not after you take into account the various overhead costs which have been left out of the deal. For example, you could be offered property which could be purchased for $50,000 and subsequently rented for $1,000. This looks like a great deal initially, but may not be quite so profitable after you include the additional taxes which will have to be paid, but have been left out of the calculations.

Some of the additional overhead costs which you will need to factor in while analyzing a potentially great deal would include income tax, property tax, maintenance fees, insurance, management fees, and community fees.

Do: Educate yourself on all options related to financing.

A wide range of financing options is available for investors to choose from, and cater to varying budget brackets. Do not limit yourself to acquiring loans from a bank or using personal finances when it comes to investing in property; explore other popular and practical options such as working with a private money lender, using hard money from an institute, or working with a fellow investor who is looking for an equity split.

As you gain ground level experience as you make more and more investments, you will find that you have developed a pattern when it comes to appreciating and analyzing a potential investment prior to making a commitment.

## BEING AN EFFECTIVE DEALMAKER – STRATEGIES TO GET YOU STARTED

A dealmaker by definition refers to someone who is adept at coordinating, negotiating, and ultimately bringing a satisfactory conclusion to all matters pertaining to commerce. In context with your experiences with real estate, you too, are aspiring to be the ultimate dealmaker. Among your many objectives are the following skills and goals:

- **Effective marketing**- You will need to learn about the various tips and tricks associated with promoting your property in a manner which grabs eyeballs and elicits a response.
- **Negotiations**- It is important to know how to maneuver your way through discussions with both buyers and sellers.
- **Locating potential buyers/sellers**- You will save time if you have an existing network of people to reach out to in the event that you are looking to buy or sell

property; this can be achieved in both, an online and offline context.

- **Know when to make or avoid making an offer**- There are a few red flags which should signal the need to avoid making an offer to a particular seller. In the same way there are some immediate green flags which indicate that the buyer/seller is right for your situation and budget.
- **Understanding the value of a seller**- The real estate market has its share of adept and trustworthy agents and realtors; in the same way it also has suspicious characters that will try and hike up prices unnecessarily, or will hide hidden costs in order to present you with a good offer. Trusting your gut instinct will go a long way in avoiding associations with sellers of ill repute.
- **Gaining knowledge regarding funding options**- Funding is an extremely important aspect of real estate, irrespective of whether you are self-funding your investment or are seeking outside help such as a loan. An entire chapter is dedicated towards exploring the various funding choices available to you, which will enable you to invest wisely without having to dig into your own finances beyond your comfort level.

Once you have understood the various areas in which you will need to inculcate both technical as well as ground level knowledge, it is time to delve into the various strategies which will facilitate a productive, i.e. lucrative real estate investing experience.

The Real Estate Market cycle illustrated below will give you a clear idea as to the overall cyclical nature of the market, enabling you to understand the various phases which your investment will experience, from the Climb to the Decline. Knowing about the existence of these phases will help you to time your investments appropriately.

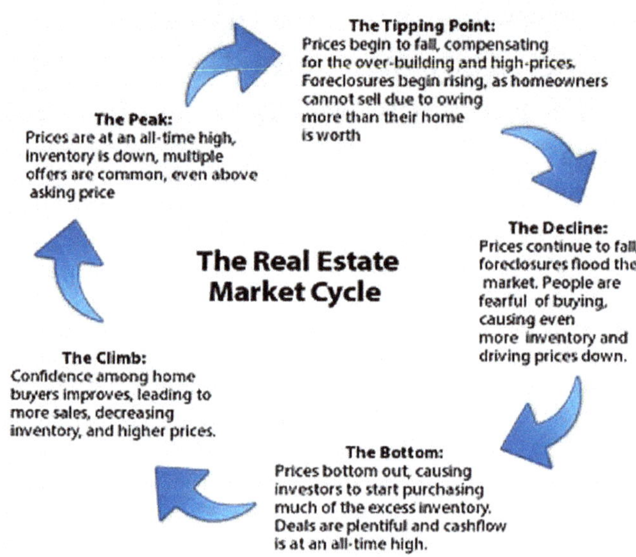


As the visual above illustrates, it is important to begin any potential investment with a clear idea as to what your exit strategy will be, in order to assure maximum profit. In other words, as an investor, you need to have options ready in context with what you are going to do after you buy a home or invest in property.

An exit strategy, by definition, refers to a plan through which an investor can cash out of an investment with the purpose of profiting from favorable market conditions, or to back out of a potentially bad market. Planning your exit strategy constitutes a vital part of your real estate investment action plan and it is important to prioritize it at the onset of a potential investment.

Another important strategy pertaining to real estate investments involves joining your local investors club in order to swap and share information with fellow investors. This will also help you in developing the "network" which was mentioned earlier in this chapter. Associating with fellow investors, individual or professional, will allow you the opportunity to gain firsthand market knowledge and could even facilitate a better investing mindset.

Enough cannot be said about the importance of sound financial planning and saving when it comes to real estate investments. It is recommended that you keep about 10-15 percent of your budget aside for the purpose of handling rehabbing and other related costs. This is especially important for investors who have scaled out to a large number of properties and are looking at flipping houses.

A tip from some of the most seasoned investors in the real estate market could very well put you on the path to earning a huge profit; focus on the millennial generation. They constitute the future of the real estate market, and are essentially "the younger generation" of people who were born between the late 80's and 90's. Focusing your investments and flipping activity in areas which are populated by (and therefore bought or rented) by them will at least ensure that your property is being viewed by potential buyers/sellers from good backgrounds. When it comes to real estate, the famed double repetition, “location, location, location” applies most aptly.

There are a number of other small but significant strategies which will help you in making informed decisions pertaining to your real estate investments. The most valuable strategy however, is to learn from ground level experience and a community of fellow investors.

The successful real estate investors realize the importance of an efficient business model. Developing a proven plan or system enhances the potential of boosting any business towards the forefront of its market.

Hence, both personal development and monetary gains can exponentially also increase through the implementation of a well-designed strategy. This also indicated that the significance of exit strategies can’t be underestimated as they are a vital part of a successful strategy.

The investors who take out some time in order to familiarize themselves with the particulars of all processes are always rewarded accordingly. On the contrary, the ones who neglect acknowledging the advantages and importance of having an appropriate exit strategy might be voided of the opportunities of achieving relevance in their industry. It is ultimately up to the investor to establish their success.

Real estate exit strategies are the strategies that help the investors to remove themselves from a real estate deal. Implementation of the right exit strategy is essential for success as the right method results in maximizing their profits and minimizing the risks.

## Importance of an Exit Strategy

In many cases, the investors fail in realizing the importance of a proper real estate exit strategy. As a result, they end up losing a lot of time and money in being stuck in deals that aren't profitable.

It is indeed true that implementation speed is rather important when an investor wants to facilitate a transaction; however, it is unwise to start a real estate deal without analyzing the possible exit strategies in order to protect yourself.

To become a successful investor, it is essential that you evaluate all possible scenarios by keeping its end in your mind. This means, that having a certain plan for all the real estate investing deals before you opt for them. You must have a clear idea about which strategy you want to use and how it can benefit you the most.

You must also familiarize yourself with all possible exit strategies that can protect you and save your business from suffering from massive losses. Many investors have lost millions of dollars only because they failed to give much importance to exit strategies.

This can even cost you your real estate investing career. It is reckless to knowingly enter negotiations without determining how you will be able to successfully exit that deal.

Such blind ambition enhances risks but also eliminate potential chances of negotiating from a position of power. It also decreases the potential profits while enhancing the risks.

## Influential Factors

The decision of determining the right real estate exit strategy to utilize isn't as simple as it might seem. There are many major factors that must be considered when you plan an exit strategy.

Eventually, the probable profitability of every deal is correlated to the particular chosen strategy. Proper understandings of every plan can assist investors in maximizing the returns on their investments.

However, there isn't any golden rule differentiating between all strategies for a single scenario. Hence, determining which exit strategy to implement depends on the investor's understandings of the following influential factors:

- Property Location
- Profit potential
- Financing options

- Demand and supply
- Property condition
- Property value
- Terms
- Purchase price
- Time to close
- Market conditions
- Level of experience
- Long and short term goals

Knowledge about all these influential factors can help the investors in determining which real estate exit must be used on the particular scenario.

## Factors That Ruins an Exit Strategy

Even though, real estate investing is a sound opportunity of making tons of money, there are many risks involved as well which must be taken into consideration by all investors. There are certain factors that can even ruin an exit strategy if the investors aren't careful. Following are some of those factors:

- Depreciation
- Poor management of property that results in reducing its value and hurting the cash flow

- Unpredicted maintenance costs which can drastically reduce or even cancel out the profit
- Lack in demand, lender backing out, or failed escrow prevents a property to get flipped
- Issues with tenants that results in lost rent

Understanding the major factors that might prevent an exit strategy being a success is essential to investors. Successful investors know the right ways of counteracting such obstacles with various strategies.

It is important to have a backup plan as anything can happen in a single moment. Having different exit strategies further lowers the impending risks and enables the investors to earn maximum returns.

## OWNERSHIP, ACQUISITION, AND KNOWING WHEN TO BUY OR HOLD

Ownership, Acquisition and knowing when to buy or hold on to your property constitute core elements of effective and ultimately profitable real estate deals. Rock bottom real estate prices may indicate towards a good time for property purchase, however you need to keep a few points in mind prior to taking a call in order to avoid bankruptcy and other unfortunate problems.

There are a number of different kinds of real estate ownership which are dependent on the type of property or the number of people who own the property. The type of ownership will extend specific legal rights and obligations, and will impact the inheritability and transferability of the property in question. It will also affect how the property will be handled in case of a dispute or bankruptcy. In specific context with real estate and individual ownership, the kind of ownership and related legalities which you will need to gain an understanding of, is Ownership in severalty. This basically means that you as the sole owner of the property are "severed" from other owners and are in a legal position to make various decisions pertaining to your property without the need to ask for consent from other parties.

You have what is technically referred to as the "Bundle of Rights"; these are a set of legal rights given to a real estate title holder, and include the following rights:

- **The right of possession**- This indicates that the property is owned by the title holder.
- **The right of control**- The use of the property is controlled by the title holder.
- **The right of exclusion**- The title holder has the right to deny access to the property.
- **The right of enjoyment**- The title holder can use the property in any legally permissible manner.
- **The right of disposition**- The title holder has the right to buy, sell, or rent the property.

The acquisition process is what follows once suitable property has been identified, and due diligence exercised (which basically involves a thorough inspection and assessment of the property in order to assess its status, value, and condition) by professionals. Usually real estate attorneys and investors are consulted, who will make you (the owner) a formal offer which includes formally confirming the desire to buy or rent your property. During this process, it is also likely that you will be offered what is known as "earnest money" which could be, but is not necessarily considered to be a down payment. This payment is an indicator of an individual's intent with regard to purchasing or renting your real estate; it will also allow the investor the right to personally inspect your property, arrange financing, and organize other prerequisites required for rental or purchase. The validity of this money and the rights it allows does have a deadline, however, and once it expires, the investor will be required to either commit or reject your property.

Buying and Holding has been touted as being one of the best ways through which to become wealthy. Buying and Holding is an investment strategy through which an investor buys real estate and does not sell it i.e. holds it for a long period of time in order to sell it during favorable market conditions.

This process however, will only rake in real profits if you pay attention to the IDEAL principle:

- **Income**- Good buy and hold investments offer positive cash flows which not only offset expenses and debt service, but will enable you to earn a monthly income.

- **Depreciation**- The value of your property can be written off after 27.5 as per the IRS; the depreciation will therefore count as negative income albeit only on paper. This is because the costs incurred in keeping the property in good condition can be covered by the amount you earn as rental income. Tax related obligations therefore, are zero; it should be noted however that this benefit can only be enjoyed by active investors.
- **Equity**- Equity will build up owing to the fact that the aforementioned cash flow will allow you to repay any existing mortgage using the rent paid by tenants. In this way you can repay an existing loan or the principle of the loan, all the while adding to the equity which you have in the property.
- **Appreciation**- In the same way as other assets, real estate too, faces its share of ups and downs and its value varies depending on variable market conditions. However, keeping in mind the history of real estate prices which have been consistently increasing at the annual rate of 4.62 percent, it can be somewhat safely stated that accelerating equity pay down (i.e. paying more principle and less interest) and appreciation will lead to an increase in your level of equity.
- **Leverage**- This refers to an investment strategy through which an investor uses borrowed money in order to benefit from outsized investment returns.

This will enable you to increase your real estate net worth.

Yes, there are many challenges in the real estate investment market. Despite these challenges, it makes a lot of sense to include real estate in your overall investment portfolio to leverage its umpteen benefits. Moreover, the challenges mentioned above are not insurmountable. With a bit of hard work, you can easily learn the tricks of the trade and rake in the moolah. Let us look at why real estate investment is one of the best ways to make money.

**Real estate deals with tangible assets** – Unlike stocks, shares, bank deposits, and some other investments, real estate deals with an asset that you can see and touch. Tangible assets are very attractive to most people. And if these assets can help you earn a secondary income, the attraction is doubled. There are many reasons to include tangible assets in your investment portfolio, and some of them are:

- Tangible assets are outside of bank accounts, exchange markets, or bank statements. They have a natural value that is derived from their physical form.
- History provides ample proof that tangible assets such as gold and bullion offer amazing protection against inflation. Although real estate returns are not at a comparable level, the need and demand for homes.

- Tangible assets give personal joy and happiness. When you see your property, there is an inexplicable joy that can hardly be measured with money. Earning income from property is secondary to many people.

**Real estate investments have short-term and long-term earnings potential** -Rental income and positive cash flows can effectively start immediately after you purchase your property.

Additionally, nearly all properties increase in value (called appreciation) over time. And, when you choose to sell your property after a few years, you can earn capital gains; the term used to refer to the difference between the selling price and cost price (which you paid many years ago). The difference in these prices can be quite significant giving you access to a great deal of money at the time of selling the property.

**Real estate investment has multiple options and strategies** – Properties come in different shapes, sizes, and options giving you amazing flexibility to choose what suits you best. You can buy residential or commercial property, single-family or multi-family homes, apartments, condos, property in rural or urban areas, farmlands, and much, much more. Each of these options can give you great returns. You can invest through partnerships, crowdfunding, or REITs (Real Estate Investment Trust), and more.

**Real estate can help in wealth generation** – Even as you work your 9-to-5 job, you can buy, own, rent out, and manage your real estate investments with each of your properties giving you rental income opportunities. Therefore, the path of real estate investments is one of the best routes to building wealth.

**Real estate investments grow on their own** – Nearly all real estate investors (those who managed their investments prudently and well) rarely stopped at one property. Within a few years of investing in real estate, most successful investors buy at least a couple more properties enhancing their stakes and earning potential in the real estate market.

For example, you can pay off your mortgages faster by using the rental income so that you can free yourself from this debt and take another one to buy your second property.

Alternately, you could save up your rental income to build enough cash balances for a down payment for a second property. The more rental properties you have with mortgages, the faster your real estate portfolio will grow.

**Real estate investments offer numerous tax benefits** – Multiple tax deductions are available with real estate investments.

**Owning real estate results in increased control over your investment portfolio** – With property, you are your own boss. All decisions regarding the property including the choice of tenants, the quantum of rent, when to buy or sell, etc. are all under your control.

The fact that you are participating in the decision-making process regarding your property makes real estate investments less risky than stocks and shares.

**Learning about real estate is not rocket science** - Most of the successful investors are people who have a regular 9-to-5 job, and yet find the time and energy to learn and manage their real estate investments. You are sure to find a couple of people in your own social circle who have managed to create immense wealth and a steady passive income through real estate investments.

Both are valid reasons, and yet, both can be easily overcome with a bit of hard work towards picking up adequate knowledge so that your fears and insecurities are handled prudently.

# CONCLUSION

Real estate investing is a path that opens up many other opportunities. If you are lagging out of fear, it will be at the cost of success. Do you want to give up on progress and good income? You wouldn't want it! Hence, you must garner all the possible information from this guide and utilize it in your investing journey.

The beginning has never been, so it is not going to be easy for you as well. As a naïve investor, you must focus on the basics. You must try to master the basics. Once you do, the rest will fall into place. Also, you shouldn't forget to keep learning because the more you learn, the better it becomes.

Even though you will be able to cover a lot from this book, it is always recommended to keep hunting for more information and knowledge. As I said, everything will be hard in the beginning, but once you get the grip, you can flaunt success.

Learning real estate can be like learning a new language for some people, but we never knew how to speak when we grew up, but then practice happened. Hence, training, learning, and experience will help you become a better investor. You have to focus on the learning procedure of investing and, eventually, you will master it!

CPSIA information can be obtained
at www.ICGtesting.com
Printed in the USA
LVHW082228200221
679507LV00003B/59

9 781914 104923